Monsters in the Mirror
Reflections on the Study of Serial Murder

Stephen J. Giannangelo

Monsters in the Mirror
Reflections on the Study of Serial Murder

Copyright © 2022 by Stephen J Giannangelo

Published by Waterfront Productions
Chicago, IL
USA

ISBN 979-8-218-00812-3

Book Layout Designer: John Borowski

Front Jacket Artwork by David Van Gough

I used to subscribe to the concept of Trent Reznor's lyric which once told me, "Everyone I know goes away in the end." At this point in life, I have found that to be often true; but Kathy, you continue to prove that it's not always the case. Thank you again.

And for my brother, Mike, who's always been there, no matter how many miles separated us.

Contents

Acknowledgements

Like any project, there were a few hands that assisted in this one. I need to mention a few:

David Van Gough, for his inspired book cover design.

Enzo Yaksic and Steve Daniels, friends and colleagues whose company and intelligence inspire everyone around them to think harder and achieve greater.

I'd like to mention works I've pulled segments of previous pieces from, and the people involved: *Serial Killer Magazine* — James Gilks; *Real Crime Magazine* — Seth Ferranti, and John Borowski's books *The Ed Gein File* and *Dahmer's Confession*.

I received inspiration and learned from many students over the years. While I'd like to mention more, I should acknowledge a few that contributed directly to this work. Thanks to Amanda Mullin, Eva Santucci, Keith Hauter, and Amy Greenan.

Ashleigh Keto for her informative words, experience and input.

Dr. Katherine Ramsland, for her gracious contribution discussing her experiences. You have always been an inspiration of mine, and this is an invaluable item.

Peter Vronsky for his generous, thoughtful gift of writing the Foreword. Peter is another mainstay to the genre whom I respect a great deal and I appreciate his memories of my earliest work.

John Borowski, for his friendship and support, help in publishing and technical advice and continued source of information, guidance, and counsel. You are a great friend, John.

And of course, Kathy Giannangelo, who I could not accomplish much of anything without. Your unwavering love and fearless support are the source of any personal goal I might accomplish.

FOREWORD

Peter Vronsky

I lived the first twenty-three years of my life blissfully unaware that there was such a thing as serial killers until I had a random brief close encounter with one on a Sunday mid-morning December 2, 1979 in New York City.

Growing up in the late 1950s-early 1960s I was aware of mythical monsters like werewolves and vampires and human 'sex maniac psychos' like Ed Gein and the Boston Strangler and everybody knew the story of Jack the Ripper; that case was only seventy-years cold when I was a child. But unlike supernatural werewolves and vampires with relatively cohesive understood modes of behavior, these human monsters were different. Each one of them was an individual, a unique complex of constantly evolving monstrosities. There was no cohesive paradigm of behavior, no species or profile category, and no understood method to their madness, not even a label that everybody agreed upon as to exactly what they were.

Even by December 1979 in the gates of the 1980s, when I had encountered my monster – "my serial killer" Richard Cottingham, the Times Square Torso Killer, creatures like the Son of Sam had already come and gone, and John Wayne Gacy, the Hillside Stranglers and Ted Bundy had been recently identified and apprehended, and by then we had already forgotten the shadowy 'multicide' monsters from the earlier 1970s like Juan Corona who buried an extraordinary twenty-five victims in a California peach orchard and Dean Corll, the "Candyman" who raped, tortured and murdered twenty-eight youths in Texas.

When I got bumped by Cottingham as he was leaving the scene of the hotel where he had tortured, murdered and beheaded two women, set the mattresses under their torsos on fire and then fled with the two severed heads in a valise, exiting the elevator into the lobby as I was entering into it to go up, there was no name for what he was or what he did. We called them all sorts of names: *psycho sex maniac multiple sequential recreational motiveless signature stranger-on-stranger pattern sexual thrill lust murderers*; or some combination of flawed and inadequate descriptors for *this thing* – that seemed to be surging at an epidemic rate since the 1960s, nested inside a baby snake nest of other things like a rise of 'ordinary murder', assassinations, race riots, domestic terrorism on both the right and left poles of the radical nether land and a war of attrition in South East Asia fought by teenage drafted conscripts.

This thing, this rising rate of pathologically repetitive, mostly compulsive sexual murders, rising like scum on three decades of shit-surges going all the way back to our grandfathers' degradation in the Great Depression of 1930s, the *totaler* Krieg rape and killing of the Second World War in Europe and the Pacific in the 1940s, and the homecoming from all that to Cold War American pulp magazine celebration of female captive torture and rape and paranoia and the births of baby boom sons like you and me in the 1950s and 1960s, and among us, damaged brother males, those few monstrous fractured Sons of Cain, raised by their cold battered mothers and abandoned by their deranged fathers and shunned and raped by their child peers and many banged up in their heads too, exiled into fantasies of revenge and control and rape and murder of our baby boom mothers and sisters and sometimes even their own.

In 1979, when I encountered "my serial killer", the only explanation available to me at the time was that I had been bumped by an Alfred Hitchcock *Psycho Frenzy* movie monster.

To make sense of what I had just experienced, one of the first books on multiple murder I turned to was Ann Rule's 1980 seminal account of Ted Bundy, *A Stranger Beside Me*. But the term "serial killer" did not appear in its pages. Not yet.

"Serial killer" was certainly a term in the constellation of terms coming into use, and there is a plausibility to the late FBI Special Agent Robert Ressler's claims that he coined it into use in the context of the psychology of movie cliff-hanger *serials* while lecturing at a police college in the UK in 1974 and that it gradually took hold first in the insular law enforcement community before being adopted in media and popular culture. That's probably how it did come to fruition, to be used the way it is used today, the term "serial killer."

For the record, the earliest (but unadopted) English-language use of the term "serial killings" I have been able to find in print was by the biblical scholar, historian and concentration-camp survivor Robert Eisler, in his annotations to a lecture he gave on sadism and anthropology to the Royal Society of Medicine in London in 1948. The lecture was published posthumously in 1951 as a heavily footnoted book entitled *Man into Wolf: An Anthropological Interpretation of Sadism, Masochism, and Lycanthropy.*

But if we are willing to accept the *New York Times* as the 'paper-of-record' then the construct 'serial murderer' and 'serial killing' first begins to appear in its pages in May 1981, to describe Wayne Williams and the Atlanta Child Murders. (M.A. Farber, "Leading the Hunt in Atlanta's Murders", New York Times, May 3, 1981.)

What exactly a serial killer might be and how to explain their genesis and existence and apprehend them was the subject of a spate of emerging articles in forensic literature with two seminal books first emerging on the subject in 1986:

> *Sexual Homicide: Patterns and Motives* by Robert K. Ressler, Ann W. Burgess, and John E. Douglas, a study with an investigative objective based on prison interviews with sexual murder perpetrators, predominately serial, conducted by FBI agent 'mindhunters' from the Behavioral Science Unit, a study on which the early generation of FBI profiling was first based;

> *Hunting Humans: The Rise of the Modern Multiple Murderer*, by anthropologist Elliott Leyton, a socio-historical study focused on the how and why of the emerging wave of serial killers since the 1960s.

In 1990 while working in Russia I randomly encountered my second serial killer (that is, that I am aware of.) Again, just like in 1979 in New York, I did not know at the time I had bumped into a serial killer until years later, when I was researching his case for what would become my first book on serial killers: *Serial Killers: The Method and Madness of Monsters.* The book when published opened with the descriptions of these two random encounters I had had.

Part of the process of writing that book was my own questioning of what the odds were for me to have randomly run into two serial killers in the way I did, and what did it say about my own life and travels, my choice of lefts instead of my rights, a question I never resolved satisfactorily. In the course of my life, I had also bumped into completely at random since a child, Robert Kennedy, Elton John, Peter O'Toole, Andy Warhol, Sammy Davis Jr., Bryan Adams, Chazz Palminteri and Yevgeny Yevtushenko. In unexpected places and situations. And four years ago, from this writing, on the day I flew into New Jersey for the first time meet in Trenton State Prison and interview "my serial killer" Richard Cottingham, I bumped into the 1980s all-girl band Bananarama at the luggage carousel at Newark Airport. Go figure out *that* math.

Where the two serial killers I met at random fit into the statistical matrix of probability and chance remains a mystery. For some, that matrix took them to death.

By the time I first sat down in 1998 to write my history of serial killers (they say, "write what you know") serial killers had already long become a celebrity 'high concept' in popular culture (like dinosaurs, baseball and UFOs). We were well into the post-*Silence of the Lambs* era of serial killer trading cards, action figures and collectible murderabilia.

I wanted to write something in between the historiographical like Colin Wilson's *A Criminal History of Mankind* and the historical narrative works of Harold Schechter and the late Michael Newton (in particular his *Rope: The Twisted Life and Crimes of Harvey Glatman.*)

As reference sources for my own theoretical inquiries, there were now available to me, in addition to *Sexual Homicide* and *Hunting Humans*, many new recently published studies, including the first edition of *Serial Murderers and Their Victims* by Eric W Hickey; Joel Norris *Serial Killers*; Robert Keppel *Signature Killers*; Ronald M. Holmes & James De Burger, *Serial Murder*; James Earl, *Catching Serial Killers*; Mark Seltzer, *Serial Killers: Death and Life in America's Wound Culture*; and Philip Jenkins, *Using Murder: The Social Construction of Serial Homicide*. These sources illuminated a variety of approaches to the thing – and how to glimpse it – but not to what it was in itself. They all attributed serial murder to other things ranging from specific diagnosed behavioral disorders, biochemistry, genetics to social constructs and even secret government brainwashing experiments. None of these sources really addressed satisfactorily a core issue: not all subjects suffering from behavioral disorders or unusual biochemistry became serial killers; in fact, only a tiny minority did. Factor X – the serial killer seed-gene-spark-atom-component, whatever it was, eluded us.

That is, except for one source that I came across: *The Psychopathology of Serial Murder: A Theory of Violence* by Stephen J. Giannangelo published in 1996. I thought it was an audacious attempt to categorize serial killing as a DSM-IV (at the time) category of its own - "Homicidal Pattern Disorder" – rather than grafting serial murder inexplicably to other behavioral disorders.

On reading Giannangelo's book today in 2022 – more than twenty-five years of serial killing later – albeit apparently less of it numerically in the United States so far – his

"Homicidal Pattern Disorder" can certainly stand further refinement and revision based on what we have learnt since then. But it was his overall notion of serial murder as a stand-alone phenomenon of its own, as opposed to as a component of other disorders, that shaped how I approached serial murder when trying to describe it as a historian when I came to write *Serial Killers*.

Now, at this writing, more than forty years after my first encounter with a serial killer, I am in the midst of what I believe is going to be my last book on serial killers: *American Werewolf: The Life and Crimes of Richard Cottingham, the Last Serial Killer on the Left*, as I have been meeting with him for four years, along with Jennifer Weiss, the daughter of one of the Torso Killing victims. In the process we have facilitated a series of recent confessions from him to law enforcement to some of the eighty to one hundred murders he claims to have committed between 1963 and his arrest in 1980. Cottingham is my alpha and omega in the underworld of serial homicide.

It was both synchronous and an honor at this watershed moment in my own exploration of serial homicide to be invited to write a foreword to this new 'state-of-the-union' collection of essays on serial murder by Stephen Giannangelo, a kind of 'mop up' of the many odds and ends and corners of serial murder from then (from when we first began calling it that) to now. Much has changed since the so-called "Golden Age of Serial Murderers", the three decades from 1970-1999, including what until recently appears to have been a dramatic but yet inexplicable decline in serial killer apprehensions since 1999. It will be as close by my side as I write my last book on this subject, much in the way his *The Psychopathology of Serial Murder* was when I wrote my first some twenty-five years ago.

Peter Vronsky, Ph.D.

Author of
Serial Killers: The Method and Madness of Monsters
Female Serial Killers: How and Why Women Become Monsters
Sons of Cain: The History of Serial Killers from the Stone Age to the Present
American Serial Killers: The Epidemic Years, 1950-2000

PROLOGUE

Echoes. A postmortem.

This book is an about-face for me. I enjoyed writing *The Psychopathology of Serial Murder: A Theory of Violence* in 1996. It was my first work, and it was a traditional, academic piece, a textbook about a subject that hadn't gotten its due. I think back to when that work was first published, decades before *ID TV* and *Criminal Minds* became staples in American entertainment, when the study of serial murder was still in its infancy. Some concepts are old hat now; others, we are still trying to figure out.

In 2012, I fulfilled a long-held wish to essentially re-write that book, updating it with all the squirrels juggling knives that were dancing in my head while studying the topic since the 80s, writing about it in the 90s and teaching about it since then. I finally was able to add the pieces to this puzzle I've wanted to address for years, including my prison interviews with a serial killer with whom I'd forged a relationship. That book, *Real-Life Monsters: A Psychological Examination of the Serial Murderer*, was cathartic and gratifying, and while still a text, was expanded and softened to include more of the casual interest people that flock to this dirty little subject of ours.

This book's contents are the echoes of this time of study and teaching. They are left over, random thoughts, to be shared with those who enjoy this topic, a post-mortem of decades of learning. They are also a continuation of a fascination with the topic, given the evolution of expert perspectives and the surrounding culture.

The book includes some discussion on some cases you've heard about, and hopefully a few that you have not. There's some topics you might agree with, and likely a couple you will argue against.

This time around, I'm writing a book for the pleasure reader. The multiple murder, repeated, predatory, graphic, gruesome, nightmare-inducing serial killer pleasure reader. Oh, there's plenty of us out there. You know who you are. I have written a long list of pieces as a free-lance author in several publications. So, it seemed pulling a few together along with some new completely unrelated random thoughts about serial murder, non-serial murder, odd cases, and abnormal violent criminal psychology as well as the vocation of teaching people about it, would make for an interesting compilation. Or it's an anthology, or a collection… feel free to argue amongst yourselves. To be fair, only a few of the chapters contain anything published previously, so, let's call it a hybrid.

I've enjoyed the opportunity to interview or query an enviable number of talented people for input in different areas of this book, offering their points of view in the areas of their expertise. It's an interesting multi-level of contribution that I am truly grateful for and appreciate a great deal. I'm very fortunate to count these contributors as friends as well as colleagues, and we all benefit from their generosity. As in my classes, I enjoy the opportunity to present different voices from my own in an attempt towards balance and interest.

This book wasn't originally intended as a textbook, but after seeing where it's landed, I can easily see it being used as one. If you are looking for a consistent direction or a goal here, don't bother. It's not done in a traditional scholarly style or designed for the classroom. But to be fair, a Serial Murder class just might find it appealing. I am kind of excited about burning the style manuals for this one. And no, there won't be a quiz. I'm putting words and images to paper that I think other ghouls like me might enjoy. I hope you agree.

CHAPTER 1

Clowns, Human Hair Spiders & Hand Tracings. Murderabilia. Who Buys this Stuff?

"Walt Disney is a mentor for me, because I've always enjoyed his creativity."

-John Wayne Gacy

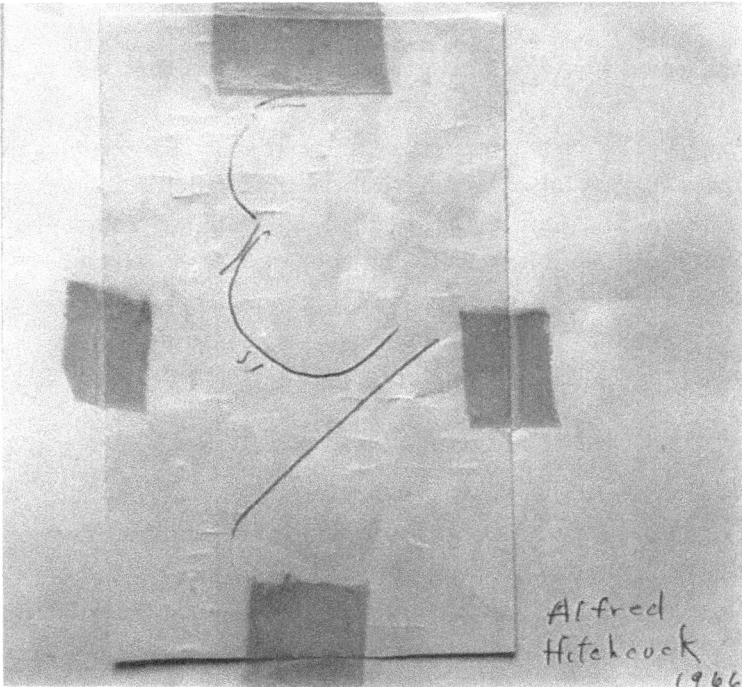

My first bit of "Murderabilia." Alfred Hitchcock's autograph from 1966. That's my mom's notation and ill-advised tape job in an old-time autograph book from the 60s. (Author photo.)

The first time I brought a painting by John Wayne Gacy into one of my university classrooms, I was met with 30 faces of abject horror. I'm going to say, it was even better than I'd hoped for.

I was looking for a way to connect something real and tangible to the very interesting but occasionally esoteric and theoretic (OK, dull) discussions we had been having in the classroom. There were plenty of eager attendees for classes like Psychology of the Offender and Serial Murder, but unfortunately, we can't *always* talk about Ted Bundy or body parts in the refrigerator.

You see, those kids in the back of the room who have their laptop/tablet/phone open with the tell-tale black mirror glow reflecting on their little faces didn't seem to know what they were missing by not paying attention to my vast dispensation of knowledge. At least the ones who sleep occasionally restrain themselves from snoring. Not loudly, anyway.

So, one night I brought in the smiling face of Pogo.

Yeah, that was a good idea.

This and other carefully chosen items over the years generated conversation that was, in my view, extremely useful and productive. The most extreme reaction was that of a woman who needed to eventually head outside in the winter cold and chain smoke every cigarette she had with her. On the other hand, this was the same student when asked to provide an article on a current case in the news that had a psychological dimension to it, generated a handful of unsolved murders in the same geographic area and said it looked like a serial killer to her. Turned out, it was. (It was Larry Bright and yes, she got extra credit!)

This topic of murderabilia is a loud and passionate one and has continued over the years with no end in sight. The names and pejoratives tossed at people who buy or collect this stuff has only been exceeded in severity by the insults hurled at those who sell them. I get it. The concern for the victims' families is real. It's understandable and expected. And some people simply find it all very distasteful.

My perspective is probably the unpopular one. When asked about this genre of collecting in John Borowski's documentary film *Serial Killer Culture*, I described the pieces as historical artifacts. I still feel that way. I cannot look at items like this, or other terribly offensive artifacts of history like Nazi symbols or Confederate flags and see them as something that should be erased from our memories. Recently, Cancel Culture has taken an ugly toehold in our society, demanding anything that might offend to be scrubbed. Of course, common decency demands they are removed from the main-stream, but as both a historical record and an educational tool? I still see usefulness.

My first purchased murderabilia, Pogo the Clown. For educational purposes only, of course. (John Borowski.)

SON OF SAM AND HIS LAWS

David Berkowitz' next door neighbor's barking dog generated one of the most famous monikers for a serial killer ever, even if the story about the dog was a lie. The nickname also carried to an early campaign against crime memorabilia and those criminals who would profit by them.

Son of Sam laws, as they were known, originated in New York in response to the idea that David Berkowitz was making money in prison from his celebrity. This was a concern that was offensive to many citizens (rightfully so) and legislation was proposed to make illegal the financial profit of one's crimes. Criminals were to be prohibited from financial benefits of writings or shows about their crimes.

The New York law was quickly enacted in 1977 after Berkowitz sold his exclusive story rights. The purpose was to "prevent those accused or convicted of a crime from profiting from the commercial exploitation of their crimes by contracting for the production of books, movies magazine articles, television shows and the like in which their crime was reenacted" or in which the "person's thoughts, feelings, opinions or emotions" about the crime are expressed.

The law directed any profits derived describing a crime to be held and made available to the victims. Other states tried to mirror New York's concept. At one point more than 40 states had Son of Sam-style laws on their books.

Unfortunately for supporters, these laws rarely withstand the Constitutional scrutiny of the First Amendment. New York lost a U.S. Supreme Court case charging Constitutional free-speech violations in a suit brought by publisher Simon & Schuster regarding a book that eventually led to the motion picture *GoodFellas*. This precedent affected other states and several lower courts have also invalidated state Son of Sam laws, including Massachusetts, Nevada, and California.

PAINTINGS, GAMES AND MORE

Of course, the most famous pieces of murderabilia are the paintings by John Wayne Gacy. Gacy forever condemned the very image of a clown to the same genre as the Universal Monsters of the 60s for many people when he started producing his paint by the numbers style renditions of himself as *Pogo the Clown* and *Patches the Clown*.

In the early 90s, I ran across this (see photo) and other flyers advertising Gacy's paintings. While the self-portraits of Pogo and Patches were the most famous, he also created "7 Dwarfs" knockoffs of the little men frolicking in the woods or other nature scenes, in different seasons, often with a potential burial site in the background. He produced all sorts of other items as well, such as pictures of famous people (John Gotti, Elvis... even Christ), and cute little birds. What pushed the enterprise ever-so-close to Son of Sam laws were the offerings of custom work and portraits being available as well. Of course, if you look closely at the flyer, there's a nod to the Son of Sam laws with the disclaimer, "John Gacy will not receive proceeds from sales." Later, he produced a book making the case for his innocence (*A Question of Doubt*) and sold a couple of book compilations of letters he wrote and received. While no one knows how much of these sales financially benefitted Gacy, the dollars realized still were not likely much at all. And in the end, it's pretty much a sure thing that he didn't take it with him to the Death House. Did they glorify him and his crimes? It's debatable. I'm not sure, but I still think burning a pile of Gacy paintings on a Chicago sidewalk after paying $20,000 for them does far more for a killer's publicity than a price list passed around a very small group of ghouls, er... potential collectors.

A little-known work by Gacy depicting the little men on a frozen pond, "Hi Ho in the Winter." (John Borowski.)

Gacy, of course, was not the only serial killer, or criminal for that matter, to produce artwork for sale. Elmer Wayne Henley, sidekick of Dean Corll, "The Candyman" from the Houston Mass Murders, was a subject in the documentary film *Collectors* starring collectors Rick Staton and Tobias Allen and is a popular seller. Danny Rolling, Clifford Boggess and many others have had their works for sale, while more and more online dealer sites have generated artwork from most every criminal you can think of and put them up for sale. Items from scorpions and spiders woven out of human hair by the late Charles Manson to hand tracings by just about everyone, it's out there for purchase.

This flyer was circulating around my Serial Murder class (that I was taking, not teaching) in 1992. $199 seemed like a lot then. (Author photo.)

Painting by Elmer Wayne Henley. (Author photo.)

Gacy's work also found its way onto music cover art as well:

Cover art for Bloody Mess & the Scabs. (Author photo.)

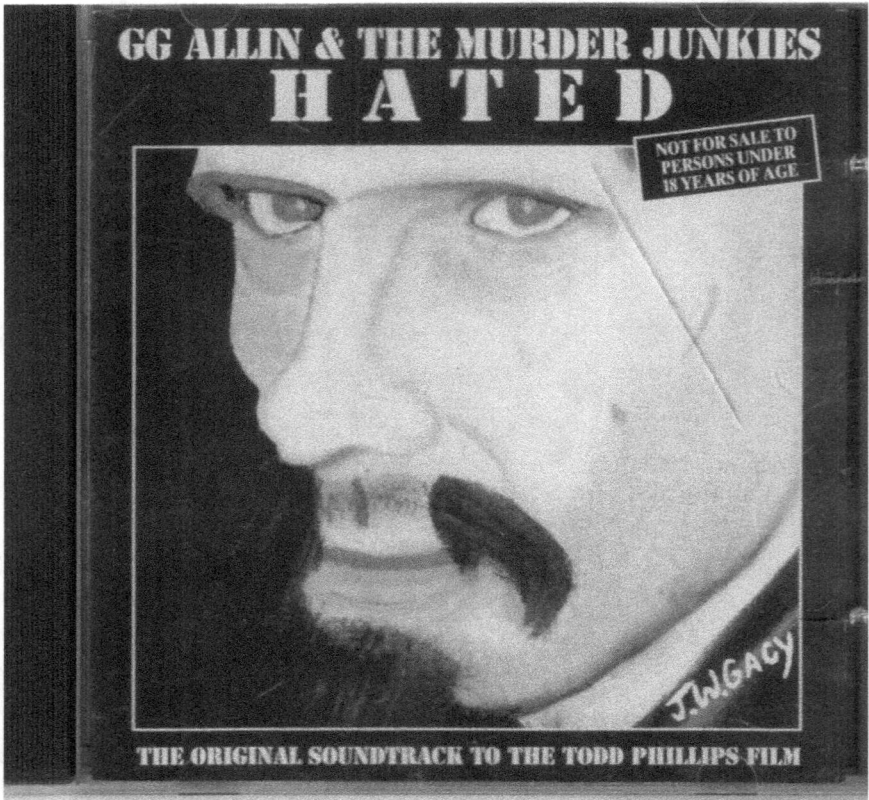

Cover art for G.G. Allin & The Murder Junkies. (Author photo.)

And of course, murderabilia has spilled over far beyond artifacts of crime scenes or personal drawings and crafts. There's been many other interesting items like serial killer board games. The first of which was a good taste-challenged adventure where players would scamper around the country trying to avoid the death penalty and accumulating money and "dead baby" tokens, which came packaged in an actual child's body bag. A later serial killer game was far more subdued, only challenging competitors to match their killer trivia skills. There's been an influx in serial killer-themed products and games in the current market, reflecting the exploding interest of anything serial killer you find streaming on TV. However, these items I show here, produced around the 90s, were much more shocking and offensive in their day's context. Not that such things aren't still offensive today.

I bought this game off eBay years ago, before they were strong-armed into a bit more restraint. Interestingly, the game was also a focal point in the aforementioned murderabilia documentary *Collectors*.

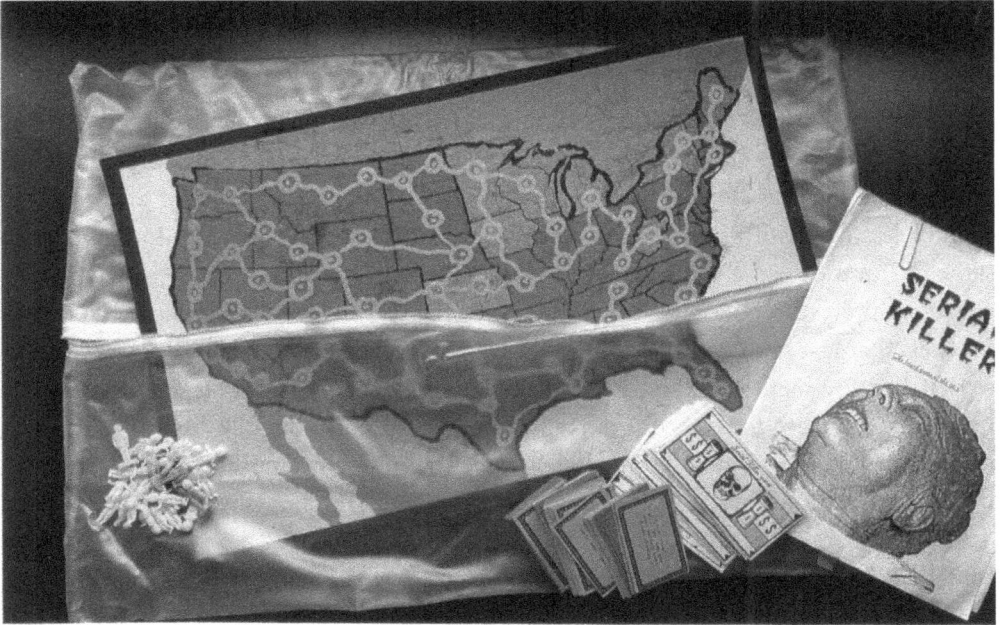

The Serial Killer board game, encased in a real child's body bag. (Author photo.)

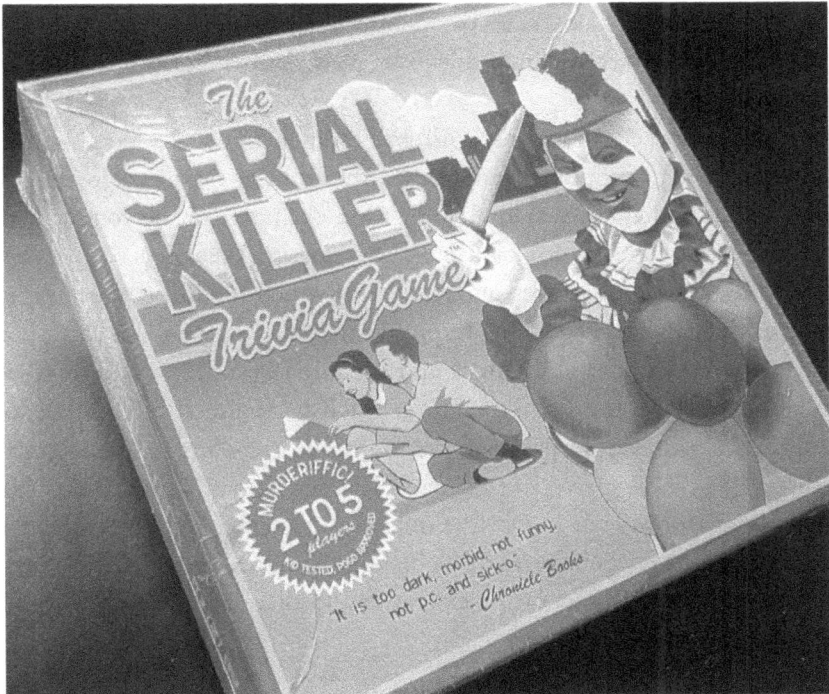

The Serial Killer Trivia Game. (Author photo.)

This doesn't include the action figures, toys and serial killer trading cards that's also managed to enrage those with much different sensitivities than this crowd.

John Borowski's 2014 documentary film *Serial Killer Culture* further explored this underbelly of murderabilia and interest in the macabre, horror and violent true crime. His later productions of *Serial Killer Culture TV* included episodes looking at this genre even closer. Many of us who grew up in a similar time frame share an interest in the same horror movies we watched as kids, and now there's a real subset of those who take an active interest in obtaining actual tokens of the real-life monsters who walk among us. (Yes, that last sentence was an intentional confluence of the titles of books by both myself and my mentor, Steven Egger. Indulge me.) The point is this country has not progressed far from the days of Frankenstein's Monster or those of Charles Manson on the cover of Rolling Stone. From slasher films to binging on multiple murderer documentary marathons. Serial Killers as an obsessive genre has not slowed in the slightest.

LETTERS, PENPALS AND PSYCHOLOGICAL ANALYSIS

Circling back to actual redeeming value of the whole world of murderabilia, it still seems there's a sliver of usefulness if you look hard enough. There's long been a segment of psychological analysis of a patient's or offender's artwork, often parsing it for hints of mental illness in both objective and subjective levels. According to Bekker & Bekker:

> …the links between an artist's work and their mental state have been examined in terms of content… more than the form of the piece, looking for a link to the individual's mental state. One example can be found in the examination of Caravaggio's painting and a potential diagnosis of paranoid schizophrenia. We are suggesting that form (which might be objective and quantifiable) can be an equally interpretive measure…. There is a correspondence between emotional intensity and the intensity of his visual representations. There have been a few studies which have aimed to correlate and quantify the paintings of psychiatric patients, by correlating color, intensity, quality of line and space covered with a patient's psychiatric disability…. Content measures such as bizarre imagery, disconnections, inappropriate or disordered color, perseveration and subject matter all require subjective interpretation on the part of the examiner and therefore are limited in objectivity.

There could be that use with serial murderers. It seems the key here first is to separate the artwork that was "directed," meaning requested, requisitioned, paid to produce or the killer was talked into producing. A painting of dancing skulls in the number of the killer's victims could evoke some reaction (and sales), but if that concept was asked of the painter, the work, while interesting, offers little in analytical value. This is true of other artificial works, such as the hand tracings I mentioned earlier. This is a simple, easy, childlike art project that any killer can churn out, sign, and maybe dabble some blood droplets across. It's certainly marketable, but in my opinion, it doesn't offer much inside to the mind of a murderer.

On the other hand, the human hair spiders by Manson… while there's not much psychological analysis going on there, this is something that he created out of his own mind and creativity and is fascinating in my view.

Gacy and Henley's paintings have been parsed and psychologically analyzed and dissected as well. The ideas of the victims being symbolically represented, the Little Men carrying digging tools emerging from the woods, the pattern of color and movement representing an entire psychological process… the idea that one character might represent Gacy himself; or that other characters could represent his reflection onto other people in their reactions… it's all very interesting and admittedly quite impossible to prove.

This brings us to serial killer correspondence. Letters have always been a fascinating peek into an offender's mind, much like artwork. From the mundane chatter of everyday talk to the darker, more descriptive moments of prose, serial killer letters have long been a subject for dissection.

The context of letters is always fascinating. What is the killer's target person? A lover? A groupie? A teacher? What does the letter-writer hope to prove? What do they want to evoke? Are they being insightful and painfully honest, or are they conning the reader and toying with them?

This letter by Ted Bundy is a favorite of mine. Obtained from a family member of one of Bundy's final attorneys, Bundy intelligently analyzes and applies the precedent and context of the 1984 case *U.S. v. Valdez*, regarding the use of hypnosis in court testimony. He believes this could affect an appeal for his convictions in Florida. A read of this truly shows the Bundy who actively participated in his own defense, sometimes acting as his own attorney and when not, being involved in the legal research and strategy. Sometimes it's easy to wonder if the brilliant, manipulative Ted was just faking his abil-

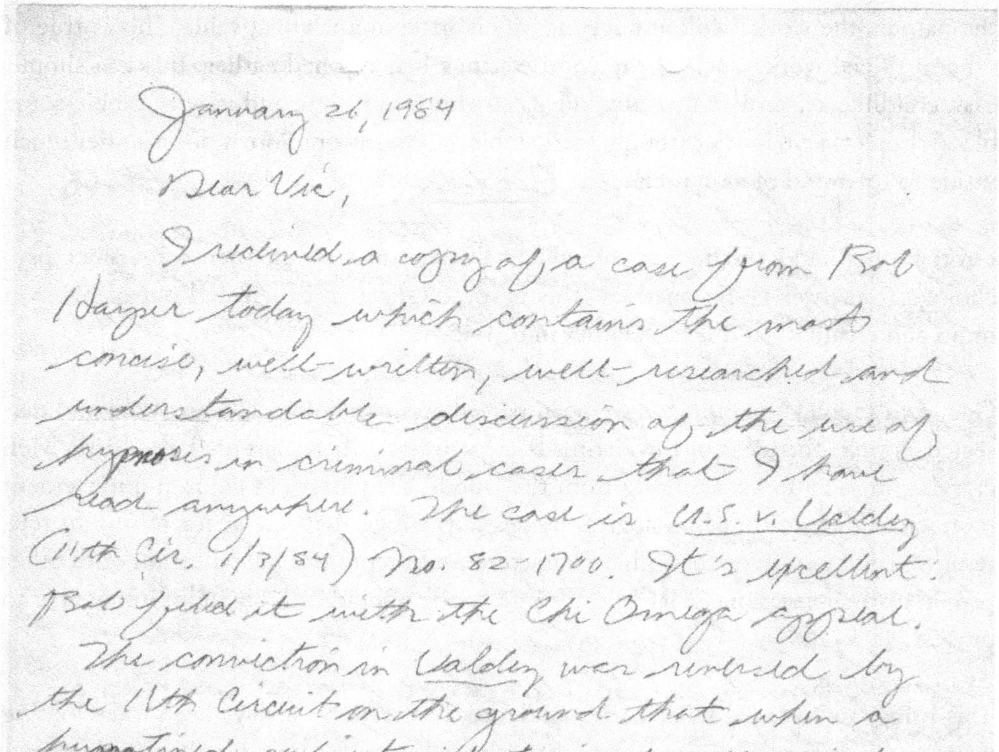

January 26, 1984

Dear Vic,

I received a copy of a case from Bob Harper today which contains the most concise, well-written, well-researched and understandable discussion of the use of hypnosis in criminal cases that I have read anywhere. The case is U.S. v. Valdez (11th Cir. 1/3/84) no. 82-1700. It's excellent. Bob filed it with the Chi Omega appeal.

The conviction in Valdez was reversed by the 11th Circuit on the ground that when a hypnotized subject identifies for the first time a person he has reason to know is already under suspicion, posthypnotic testimony is inadmissible, whatever procedural safeguards were used to attempt to sanitize the hypnotic session.

Valdez all-but mandates a reversal in the Leach case, sooner or later, if it holds up. Of course, even before Valdez

REC'D JAN 30 1984

Letter by Ted Bundy, written to one of his attorneys. (Photos by Author.)

-2-

things were looking good on the hypnosis issue.

Have you read Valdez? Do you think you need to file it in the Slack appeal? If you do, I would suggest pointing out to the Florida Supreme Court, briefly, how similar Valdez is factually and how the ruling in Valdez creates a strong precedent in the Slack case.

How are you? How is Paul? Merry Christmas. We didn't send out cards this year. Please give my best regards to your family. Carol and Rosa and Jamie are doing fine. So am I.

Take care

peace
Joe

ity to participate actively, even at a technical level, in his own defense. But letters such as this, written in good faith and in earnest while trying to assist his attorney, simply prove that Ted did in fact have the ability to work within the legal system. If he could have resisted killing scores of women, that is.

The letter rolls away from the legal points and urgency of the moment and veers off to a closing of "we didn't send out Christmas cards this year... Take care, Ted." Typical Ted.

I'd have to describe my most extreme bit of killer crime collectible as the John Wayne Gacy paint kit:

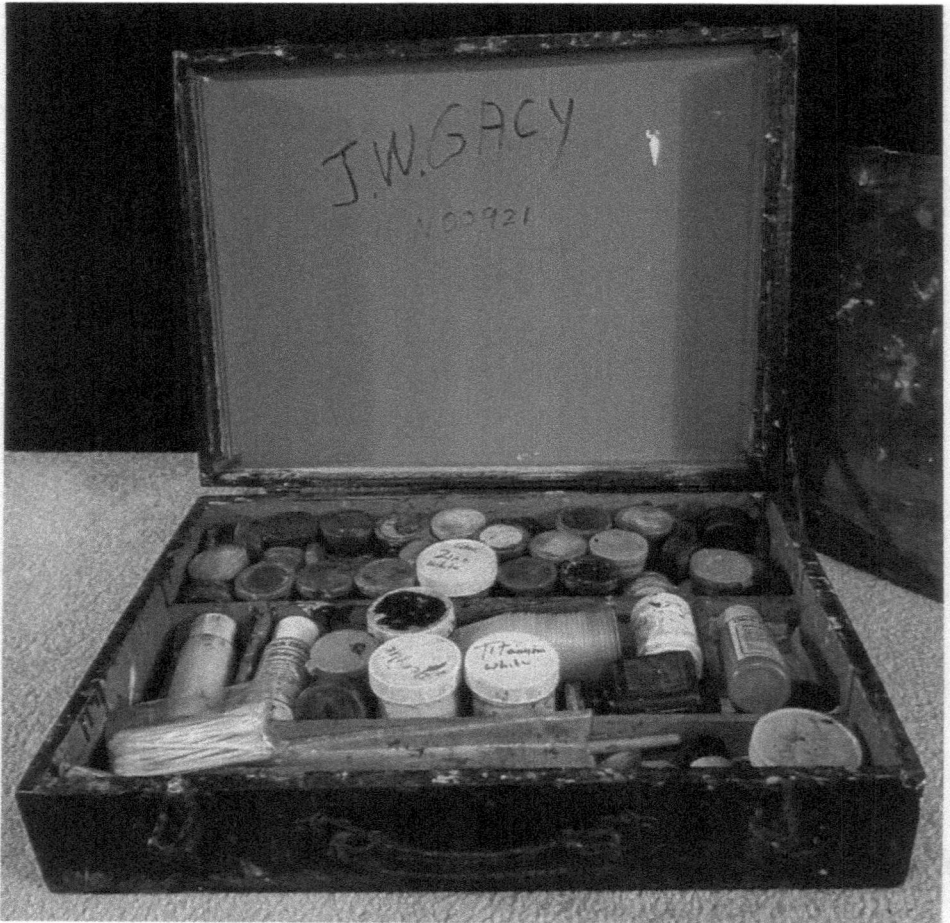

Paint kit used by John Wayne Gacy. (Author photo.)

I think it generates the most discussion of any item I've owned and displayed.

EERIE EXHIBITS

Museums that house the most extreme in true crime memorabilia have always been successful draws for the public. The Museum of Death in Hollywood, California, (a location reportedly moving) and New Orleans, Louisiana have always been popular destinations for aficionados, as was the National Museum of Crime and Punishment in Washington, DC when it was located there and as well at its most recent home in Pigeon Forge, Tennessee under the name Alcatraz East Crime Museum. It is interesting that one of the notable success stories during the recent pandemic was The Graveface Museum, who opened their doors on Valentine's Day 2020, weeks before the shutdowns that crippled so many other businesses, large and small. Towards the end of the year, things were so "grave" that the business was in danger of closing like so many others.

But in a fortuitous twist, a video posted by a TikTok user covering a visit to the museum went viral and suddenly a new large group of people found the scary locale a welcome respite from the daily horrors of 2020 and 2021, a nonstop amalgamation of ultra-hyper politics, social unrest, and new virus strains.

The different world the viewer is transported to in the quirky, creepy museum located in the "sleepy tourist town of Savannah" (description by owner Ryan Graveface), was (and is) just the diversion many people craved.

MURDERABILIA AS A TEACHING AID

Given that much of this book is presented in the context of teaching, it's important to view the collection, display, and discussion of these artifacts in that perspective. Possessing and discussing these items are not glorifying or condoning anything. Along with the established clinical analysis established by professionals reviewing art and correspondence, other items serve this purpose as well.

Years ago, I made a trip to London, England, where I of course found the need to partake in one of the popular "Jack the Ripper walks," a late-night tour in the neighborhoods where Jack prowled and stalked his prey. Our guide expertly explained the murders at each location and dramatically read from some of the letters attributed to Jack, (correctly or falsely) and provided useful, informative commentary.

However, I asked the guide where these letters were housed. He stated they were at the famous "Black Museum" (AKA the Metropolitan Police Museum) at New Scotland Yard. Of course, I asked if anyone could visit. At that time, I was told that it was used as a teaching collection for Police recruits and only credentialled law enforcement officers could go. (Unless you were some sort of VIP which quickly eliminated me) Fortunately, I was still an active law enforcement officer with my credentials in hand, so it took just one phone call, and I had an appointment to visit the next day. I found this to be terribly interesting and informative and I was treated kindly and professionally by the staff. We had a lively conversation about the contents there, including the bathtub used by serial killer Dennis Nilsen to cut up bodies and other artifacts of murderers and cannibals. The Jack the Ripper items and letters were a magnet of course, as was a discussion about just who Jack really was and what letters, if any, were believed to be authentic. It was an experience that doesn't come along often.

In his book, *Murderabilia*, Steven Scouller discusses the Black Museum and interviewed the late Curator Alan McCormick, a fine professional I also spoke with. A key point relevant to this chapter made by McCormick and reported by Scouller: "if you don't learn from the past, you will never learn at all. When you talk about using artifacts for teaching lessons, that's what this is."

That is what all this is.

SEEING THE OTHER SIDE

While I've always taken the position that murderabilia doesn't really hurt anyone, that it's historical and informative and the killers aren't exactly getting rich off them especially if they are dead, I have been exposed to the other side.

I've always rejected offers of letters from terrorists as I frankly don't need to analyze what they are thinking. I've never found them or their thoughts terribly deep, whether they are foreign or domestic. Disillusioned. Blow stuff up, kill people. Look how powerful I am. Not interested.

My career in law enforcement dulls any interest in cop-killer items, as well.

However, I remember a story about a nurse who was fired in Houston after asking for an autograph from a murderer who shot a Police officer 15 times from behind. Her weak, lame excuse was typical of someone trying to cash in on the notoriety of a murderer, in this social media, fame- obsessed world. As a retired law enforcement officer,

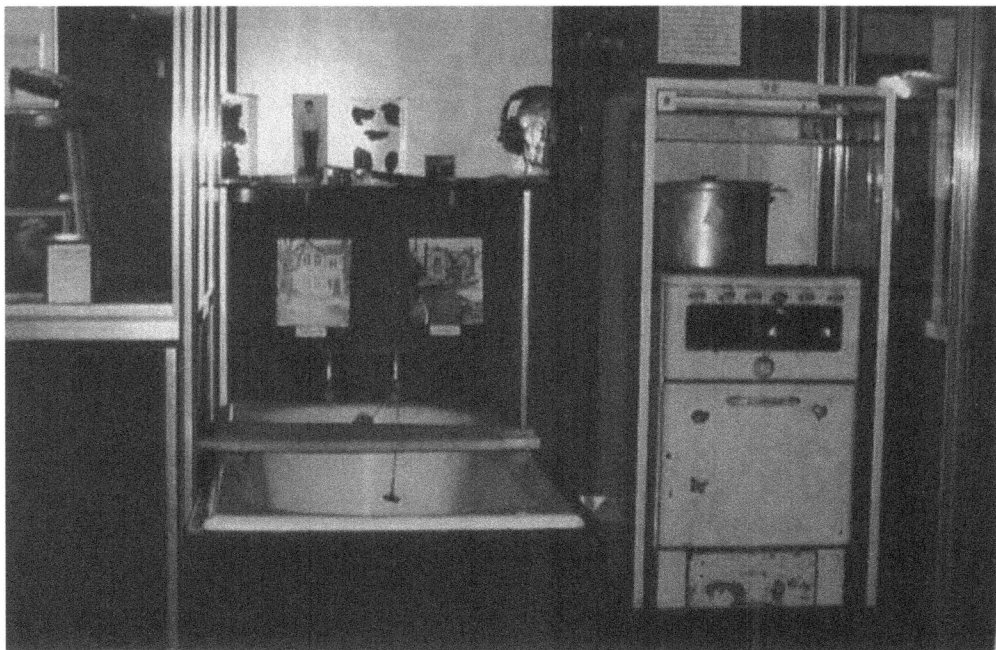

Articles removed from the home of UK killer Dennis Nilsen, housed at New Scotland Yard. (Author photo.)

I've always been personally revulsed at those who murder cops just because they think they are proving something besides cowardice. While I've never been related to a murder victim, this was as close to experiencing the outrage a victim's family member might feel when he or she hears of someone selling such items, cashing in on the horrific act against a loved one. This perspective certainly causes me pause in this topic, and further reflection.

I recently was involved in a debate with a person who sells quite a bit of this distasteful stuff, but who at the same time was making a very loud commentary against those who sold Nazi items. He took a great deal of offense to the idea that some people sold these items. I was taken aback, as I could not help but ask, "you think Nazi artifacts are somehow too offensive for anyone to sell or own due to ethical concerns, yet you sell items owned by men who tortured and raped women and killed people for fun? Or items related to terrorists? Or cop killers?"

But the fact is, he's Jewish. Nazi items were on a different plane to him. It put me in that place of thinking that cop killer items are in a different place to me, and in turn makes us further understand why anyone related to victims of violent crime might take offense to any of this stuff. I'm still strongly resistant to anyone who might try to restrict sales or ownership of any historical pieces of evidence of the worst of humanity, even the ones that bother me, but I'm further reminded of the limits we place on ourselves. In the eventual debate that bringing these artifacts in to class generates, which of course is the point of it all, I'm reminded of a comment made by a student who didn't say much in that class, but made it count when he did.

He noted that "I find it hard to believe there are still people in this room debating whether it's right to collect and be interested in this stuff when they are sitting in a Serial Murder class with this textbook in their hands."

From the mouths of babes.

REFERENCES

Bekker, K.G. & Bekker, A.Y. (2009, December 15). Color and emotion- a psychophysical analysis of Van Gough's work. *PsyArt, an online Journal for the Psychological Study of the Arts*. https://psyartjournal.com.

Collectors, a film by Julian P Hobbs. (2000). www.abjectfilms.com.

Ferris, Jan. (1994, June 19). Gacy's art is torched amid cheers. *Chicago Tribune*. www.chicagotribune.com.

Fordahl, Matthew. (1994, May 14). Art buyer plans to burn Gacy paintings. *AP News*. https://apnews.com.

Molinet, Jason. (2015, September 3). Autograph-seeking jailhouse nurse fired over alleged Texas cop-killer murderabilia flap. *New York Daily News*. www.newyorkdailynews.com.

Scouller, Steven F. (2010). *Murderabilia and true crime collecting*. Central Milton Keynes, UK. Author House.

Serial Killer Culture. A John Borowski Film. (2014). Waterfront Productions.

Serial Killer Culture TV. Season 1. A John Borowski Show. (2017). Waterfront Productions.

Serial Killer Culture TV. Season 2. A John Borowski Show. (2018). Waterfront Productions.

Spitznagel, Eric. (2021, October 30). Museum devoted to serial killers and cults is pandemic's hot tourist spot. *New York Post*. https://nypost.com.

U.S. v. Valdez. (1984, January 3). 722 F. 2d 1196. #82 1700. U. S. Court of Appeals. 5th Circuit.

Vann, Sonya C. (1994, May 18). Owner will turn Gacy's art to ashes. *Chicago Tribune*. www.chicagotribune.com.

CHAPTER 2

Jeffrey Dahmer; a Broken Mind or Broken Soul?

"It's a process, it doesn't happen overnight, when you depersonalize another person and view them as just an object. An object for pleasure and not a living human being. It seems to make it easier to do things you shouldn't do."

-Jeffrey Dahmer

Jeffrey Dahmer. (1991, Milwaukee, USA. Allan Y. Scott/AP/Shutterstock.)

In January 1992, as a graduate student looking to integrate the psychology of the serial killer with clinical and abnormal psychology, I took a course called Serial Murder. The course was taught by international serial murder expert Dr. Steven Egger, and I probably never enjoyed another class as much.

A few months earlier, it was reported that a man in Milwaukee, Jeffrey Dahmer, had been arrested and was accused of being a serial killer, and he was found to have had skulls and bones and body parts in his apartment. It was said he was a cannibal. He had body parts, two hearts and a bicep, in his refrigerator that Dahmer said he "planned to eat" later. Dahmer said he "ate only the people he really liked," according to Police.

The news, over and over, played the video of the blue vat of acid used to decay the remains of his victims, being removed from his home on a cart.

Not long afterwards, a contact I had from the Milwaukee PD provided me a copy of the killer's confession and crime scene photos. The details were stunning. The pictures, mesmerizing. These documents are widely available today, but on this day were unheard of. The media saturation of the criminal trial was in full swing during my time in class, and the confession was an amazing connection to the killer himself.

I used the Dahmer case study as an early centralized point of focus when working on my master's thesis. At one point, I attempted to contact Dahmer with inquiries and surveys in order to develop a relationship for an interview. These materials were returned to me by the Department of Corrections in Wisconsin as they were considered "contraband" because I'd included a return envelope with a stamp. Who knew? Sadly, Dahmer was murdered before I had the chance to re-send the materials and establish contact.

This was my introduction to Jeffrey Dahmer. I have always found his case, his mindset, his personality, to be fascinating. I still do.

It would be arrogant and unreasonable to purport to offer a psychological profile on a subject I've never spoken to. I would not be qualified to do that anyway. This essay is merely one person's observation and reactions to the mind and motivations of one of the most memorable serial murderers to this day.

DEPARTMENT OF CORRECTIONS
Division of Adult Institutions
DOC-243 (Rev 03/90)

WISCONSIN
ADMINISTRATIVE RULE
CHAPTER DOC 309

NOTICE OF NON-DELIVERY OF MAIL

INTENDED RECEIVER

NAME	INMATE NUMBER (if applicable)	INSTITUTION (if applicable)	
Dahmer, Jeff	177252	001	
ADDRESS - Street or P.O. Box	CITY	STATE	ZIP CODE
P O Box 900	Portage	WI	53901

SENDER

NAME(and Company Represented by Sender, if applicable)	INMATE NUMBER (if applicable)	INSTITUTION (if applicable)	
Steve Giannangelo			
ADDRESS - Street or P.O. Box	CITY	STATE	ZIP CODE
3/13 Elmhurst Dr	Springfield	IL	62704

NON-DELIVERY INFORMATION

DATE ITEM POSTMARKED	ITEM REJECTED FOR DELIVERY (Letter, Package, Magazine, Book, ETC.)
8-19	1 Stamped Env.
or DATE ITEM RECEIVED	
8-23	

REASON FOR NON-DELIVERY

☐ MAIL PRIVILEGES BETWEEN THE ABOVE INDIVIDUALS HAVE BEEN SUSPENDED.

☑ ITEM CONTAINS CONTRABAND.

☐ ITEM THREATENS CRIMINAL ACTIVITY OR PHYSICAL HARM TO A PERSON.

☐ ITEM THREATENS BLACKMAIL OR EXTORTION.

☐ ITEM CONCERNS SENDING CONTRABAND IN OR OUT OF THE INSTITUTION.

☐ ITEM CONCERNS PLANS TO ESCAPE.

☐ ITEM CONCERNS AN ACTIVITY WHICH, IF COMPLETED, WOULD VIOLATE THE LAWS OF WISCONSIN, THE UNITED STATES OR
        THE ADMINISTRATIVE RULES OF THE DEPARTMENT OF CORRECTIONS.

☐ ITEM IS IN CODE.

☐ ITEM SOLICITS GIFTS FROM A PERSON OTHER THAN A FAMILY MEMBER OR A PERSON ON INMATE'S VISITING LIST.

☐ ITEM IS OBSCENE.

☐ ITEM CONTAINS INFORMATION, WHICH IF COMMUNICATED, WOULD CREATE A CLEAR DANGER OF PHYSICAL OR MENTAL
        HARM TO A PERSON.

☐ PUBLICATION WAS NOT RECEIVED, IN ITS PACKAGE, DIRECTLY FROM THE PUBLISHER OR ANOTHER RECOGNIZED
        COMMERCIAL SOURCE.

☐ PUBLICATION TEACHES OR ADVOCATES BEHAVIOR WHICH VIOLATES THE LAWS OF WISCONSIN, THE UNITED STATES OR THE
        RULES OF THE DEPARTMENT OF CORRECTIONS.

☐ PUBLICATION TEACHES OR ADVOCATES VIOLENCE AND PRESENTS A CLEAR AND PRESENT DANGER TO INSTITUTIONAL
        SECURITY.

☐ PUBLICATION TEACHES OR DESCRIBES THE MANUFACTURE OR USE OF WEAPONS, EXPLOSIVES, DRUGS, OR INTOXICATING
        SUBSTANCES.

☐ PUBLICATION TEACHES OR DESCRIBES THE MANUFACTURE OR USE OF DEVICES WHICH CREATE A SUBSTANTIAL DANGER
        OF PHYSICAL HARM TO OTHERS.

SIGNATURE OF INSTITUTION STAFF MEMBER	DATE SIGNED
	8-23-94

IMPORTANT	PLEASE NOTE	IMPORTANT

IF YOU DISPUTE THIS DECISION, YOU HAVE THE RIGHT TO APPEAL TO THE SUPERINTENDENT BY SUBMISSION OF A WRITTEN COMPLAINT

DISTRIBUTION: Original - Security Director   Copy - Inmate Personal Property File   Copy - Sender   Copy - Intended Receiver

A violation notice from Columbia Correctional informing me that they did not deliver the
"contraband" I sent to Jeffrey Dahmer. (Author photo.)

CHILDHOOD

Jeffrey Dahmer was born in 1960 in Milwaukee, Wisconsin. His childhood fascination with dissection, animal bones and carcasses are well-known. He would collect roadkill and bring them home to dismember, examine and store away. It's hard to ignore this in context with his later behavior as an adult. His early fixation with the inner workings of the animals carried right up to his placing his ear to a victim's stomach to hear the sounds inside.

Jeff always seemed to exhibit a lethargic attitude about most everything, noted by class-mates and others alike. He appeared extremely painfully introverted, although there were moments when he acted out in ways that made people remember him. It seemed he really didn't know who he was.

His underachievement, even in activities he demonstrated some success in, was an on-going theme: through childhood, young adulthood, the military, a vocational school he never attended. His very lack of motivation and drive underscored his belief he would fail again. Certainly, with a potential lover. It's not shocking he would retreat deep into a fantasy world of rehearsing an event that would bring him the ownership of another person in the way he most desired.

It should be noted when he returned from prison for child molestation in 1990, it was rumored he'd been the victim of a sexual assault, which was unsubstantiated. However, his stepmother Shari stated that, "he'd lost his soul in there" and that he no longer had light in his eyes.

INFLUENCE OF HIS PARENTS

Along with Dahmer's interest in body parts and his ongoing distress over his sexuality and lack of success with sexual partners, it seems the biggest influence in his mindset came from his parents.

His mother, Joyce, was a high-anxiety, stressed woman who never met a conflict she didn't like. She demanded attention and courted drama. She suffered from various psychological and physical maladies, including an unexplained form of "rigidity" to her body, months before Jeffrey's birth. She had at least one suicide attempt. It was always difficult to differentiate her illnesses from what appeared to be orchestrated performances.

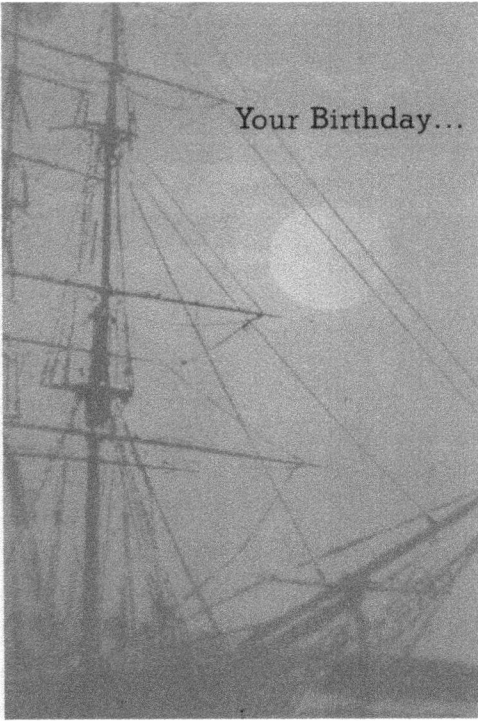

Your Birthday…

…a day to dream on
…a day to enjoy
…a day to remember!

Happy Birthday ///

My Dearest Barbara,
May your special
day be filled with joy
and every good thing!
all my love,
XOXOXO! and very Hugs!

A birthday card sent by Dahmer to a pen pal. (Author photo.)

The most obvious prenatal concern was her addiction to medications to address her many physical and emotional maladies. Joyce Dahmer was reportedly taking as many as 26 pills a day at the time she delivered Jeff. It's difficult to determine the effect this prenatal exposure had.

Jeffrey's father, Lionel, had his own influence on Jeff's development. Lionel has taken on a personal responsibility for Jeff's outcome in interviews and in his own book. Lionel, as a young boy had his own destructive interests and violent fantasies and once bombed a child off a bike with explosives. Would these natural instincts towards violence be something he could have passed on and might have addressed with his son? It seems the only thing Lionel taught his son as a child was the chemical bleaching of animals' bones, something that would serve him later in the preservation of human skulls and skeletal remains.

The most critical influence, however, seems to be the combined trauma both parents delivered with their contentious, selfish, and angry divorce and more importantly, their abandonment of Dahmer and his little brother in the house at age 18. This final brutal, abject rejection was not inconsistent with the mutual neglectful lack of attention they paid their son, something he always carried with him. While it's true this act might not have affected all young men like it did Dahmer, the loneliness and isolation was a factor in his personality that shaped his actions to come. Different sorts of trauma affect people in diverse ways, and this act was as significant as it was devastating to Jeffrey.

HIS CRIMES

Jeffrey Dahmer murdered at least 17 men and boys by 1991. His crimes are legendary. His first murder was in response to a potential sexual partner who wanted to leave. Most of the later murders involved an attempt at obtaining and controlling a subservient partner who would never leave. He drilled holes and poured chemicals in a victim's skull in an experiment in trying to create a sex zombie. Committing necrophilia with a victim's corpse was a perfect solution to the complete control Dahmer required in a partner. And finally, the act of cannibalism, was the ultimate act of control and ownership of another human being, one who would never leave him. The dismemberment that came with this act, while later described as distasteful by Dahmer, was an essential intimate prelude.

PSYCHOLOGICAL OBSERVATIONS

Dahmer's history is briefly summarized in order to provide a short background to his road to madness. Dahmer was reportedly diagnosed with several clinical conditions, including borderline personality disorder, antisocial traits, schizotypal personality disorder and psychosis. It's also reasonable to infer a degree of narcissism, obsessive-compulsive behavior, and a reasonable degree of psychopathy. There's also an apparent childish emotional lack of development that's hard to overlook, as well as the suggestion of attachment disorder.

Dahmer seemed to suffer from depression throughout his adult life along with loneliness at a terrible level. He exacerbated his problems with alcohol abuse, unsuccessfully self-medicating and facilitated his crimes with the intentional use of alcohol to reduce his inhibitions. He eventually confessed to a psychiatrist that he felt he could commit the crimes without the alcohol.

Dahmer's pathology stemmed from a severe intertwining of his extreme sexual desire of a very specific physical homosexual type, in a completely subservient role, along with a deep interest in bodily function, structure and the dismemberment of the human body. Dahmer's motivation in dismemberment cannot be dismissed as a mere attempt at hiding and disposing of victims' bodies. This connection with his childhood fascination with animal body parts and sexual stimulation is clear.

At trial, Dahmer's defense team attempted to connect his murders with an irresistible impulse connected with his desire for necrophilia. They also tried to infer his horrific acts could only be committed by someone controlled by a mental disease. The prosecution's star expert witness could not discount the existence of a mental disease, but blamed his behavior on an absence of character, and insistently offered his capability for self-control was evidenced by his ability to effectively lie when caught and to proactively avoid detection.

INSANITY

Dahmer's case, like many serial killers before him, came down to an unsuccessful insanity defense. To be fair, it's probably the only way one can describe the multiple killings, torture, dismemberment, and cannibalism he committed. The behavior seems to describe itself. Of course, it's crazy. Isn't it?

However, as with most other insanity defense cases, it wasn't an excuse a jury was willing to accept. And on the surface, it almost seemed esoteric to attempt to find this multiple killer insane. He'd admitted his crimes. He begged for forgiveness in open court from the victims' families and from God. He stood there barely interested when one victim's family member appeared to attempt to assault him in open court. It did seem hollow, though, as Dahmer read his prepared statement in the same dull expressionless monotone that he'd mumble to his father when explaining his latest failure. Remorse? Who knows?

The end game here was to keep him out of prison's General Population where he'd be a high interest target. It was a worthy goal. It was here where Dahmer met his final punishment, beaten to death by a fellow inmate for motivations truly known only by his self-appointed executioner.

AN ANSWER?

Dahmer's mental defects were many. His deep depression and abject loneliness seemed to mentally immobilize him. He seemed resigned to failure, rejection, and disdain from others. His body language, affect and manner of speaking gave the impression he was taking medication; something that probably might have helped him along with therapy if given the opportunity. This was replaced by alcohol in his daily routine of self-medication. Dahmer, like Bundy, Gacy and other serial killers, reached a point in his life where he understood that there was a compartmentalized segment of his psyche that included the need to habitually murder other human beings in order to own them the way he needed to. This may have tortured him, but he had no intention to stop at the time Tracy Edwards ran to Milwaukee Police with handcuffs dangling from his wrist that night.

It's hard to rank and assess the various factors in Dahmer's life that brought him to that moment, the night of his arrest. I must believe the breaking point was the abandonment of his parents, which left him rocking and chanting and moaning to himself, trying to speak to the dead, much like he was described years later by a would-be victim just before he attempted to take another life.

I tend to agree with the Prosecution's expert, Park Dietz, when he likened Dahmer's case to one of a pedophile. He might have liked to stop, but he didn't. His enjoyment of killing innocent men and having sex with their lifeless bodies was too great. His selfish personal need and desire to own their bodies and defile them was more important than those people's rights to live. Jeffrey Dahmer's decision seems like a sane one, however insane it sounds to the rest of us.

(NOTE: much of this essay was originally published in John Borowski's 2016 book *Dahmer's Confession*)

AN UNDEVELOPED RESOURCE

An interesting source of information and development regarding Dahmer has always been his father, Lionel. Dahmer certainly was impacted by several factors that played into his development as a serial killer, not the least of which included his mother's pre-natal prescription drug regimen, his loneliness, alienation, and anxiety based on his awkward personality and struggles with personal sexuality.

However, the insight offered by his father in his 1994 book, *A Father's Story*, offered a glimpse into a development process few serial murderers have in their case histories. The details of the book take the reader through Lionel Dahmer's attempts over the years in trying to set his son straight and on a different path, although he had absolutely no conception of what his son was capable of. Just a general foreboding of a dark ending.

The striking information about Lionel's personal history, and the way it was compared to Jeffrey, is startling. Lionel revealed a childhood obsession with fire. It drifted and developed into a fascination with bombs and explosives. He nearly accidentally burned down a neighbor's garage at one point. While he noted this interest could have led to a disastrous attachment to his developing sexuality, it seemed it had led to nothing more significant than Lionel's future emphasis in chemistry.

Lionel, as a child, experienced a paralyzing shyness, dreading to move up in grade each year and avoiding people while considering the world as "hostile and suspicious." The eerily similar terrors and feelings of inferiority and inadequacies that Jeffrey encountered as a child were a stark reminder. Lionel said that "noting his (Jeff's) fear of school, his awkwardness and lack of friends, it struck me that he had probably inherited this same dread" from his father.

It's interesting reviewing Jeff's childhood and coming to appreciate the pure terror he had of other people at one point. While Dahmer is well-known for wanting to possess living sex zombies and later settling for necrophilic acts, it's generally understood that he did not want to be alone, at a pathological level. This fear of abandonment was also shared by his father as a young man. But beyond that, his history suggests that he was so intimidated and threatened and unable to relate to other people at the simplest of levels, a trait that he seems to have inherited from his father, that his partners needed to be deceased for him to lie with them and feel comfort. A trait that, unlike his father, he was unable to cope with and control. This is an essence to Dahmer's personality that is underappreciated.

Lionel also recalled a need to find strategies to "hold things forever" and "keep them permanently within my grasp." This pathological need for permanence and control was directly recognizable in Jeff's desire to own and keep bodies, body parts and to commit the ultimate form of control… cannibalization. Every facet of Jeffrey Dahmer's needs was to enjoy complete control, including no existence of the other person's needs or desires. Others were reduced to a functioning being simply to serve Jeff's needs from listening to stomach sounds to his sole sexual gratification.

After listening to the psychiatric evaluation of his son in court, Lionel began to realize the existence of these feelings in his history. One story he would tell was of a girl named June who Lionel brought to his room around age 13. He attempted to practice hypnosis on her, to completely control her, as a manner of control Jeff would later try on his sex zombies.

Part of this developed from Lionel's overwhelming feelings of inadequacy and weakness in high school. After many experiences and strategies, he gravitated towards making bombs. As I mentioned earlier when Lionel moved on from an interest in fire to explosives, he created a concoction of chemicals that created an explosive that he used to blow a boy off a bicycle. Another time he created a small bomb that was set off in the school, providing the elder Dahmer with a great feeling of power and newfound control.

Lionel Dahmer described these actions as created within a "dark mood." It came from a need to assert himself and his willingness to use this power was a way to "let the world know I was not to be trifled with, that I was not the weak, skinny runt they imagined me to be."

These shared feelings with Jeffrey are formidable. Lionel was not far from committing a violent act on the right day and set of circumstances. We can say that Lionel learned to control his impulses and insecurities and matured, but the more you read his father's psychological background and behaviors, the degrees of separation of father and son were fewer than anyone imagines.

Shari and Lionel Dahmer. (1992, Milwaukee, USA Rick Wood/AP/Shutterstock.)

AN UNSUBSTANTIATED REPORT

In my years researching Dahmer some interesting items have come up. In one witness interview, an individual told me a story about a sighting of Dahmer not far from West Allis, Wisconsin, the location of Jeffrey Dahmer when he stayed with his grandmother. The gist of this story was that this person and a family member reported seeing Jeffrey Dahmer, months before his arrest, driving in a small red pickup truck. Part of this account included the report that Dahmer was in the company of an "older man" in the passenger seat. Jeffrey Dahmer was reportedly driving.

Reportedly the family member was 10 years old when the incident occurred and was quite sure it was Dahmer. This strong belief is shared by the reporting party. I did not at any time speak to the family member who was a child at the time.

The reporting party said the pickup truck was seen driving towards the young family member, who was walking with a friend. They ran away. The vehicle appeared to follow them around the building. They sped up, then left. Police were called and the reporting party saw him again in the red pickup truck, in a parking lot. The reporting party walked towards the men and "stared him down" and the driver would not look back. No license plate number was gathered. When the driver was seen the second time it was from about 10 feet away and the older man was present in the pickup.

This event happened in 1990 and they remembered it "was cold out." The family member, a fifth grader, eventually saw a picture of Jeffrey Dahmer in the newspaper. This person also saw him on TV news after his arrest in 1991. At that time, they identified the driver of the truck as Dahmer. The family member has reportedly never discussed any of this with the friend who was walking with them at first.

The name/ location of these events is unclear, described as a city/town "about 30 minutes from West Allis."

As I looked at a general activity timeline for Dahmer, I came up with this general overview just as a guide for comparison:

-After being discharged from the military for alcoholism, Jeff landed in Florida for awhile
-He returned to Ohio to live with his parents, had trouble with drinking and run- ins with Police, and was sent to visit with his grandmother in West Allis, WI in 1981
-Dahmer lived with his grandmother for over 6 years into the late 80s in West Allis, WI, then in an apartment beginning in 1988
-Was arrested for indecent exposure in 1982 and '86, then arrested for drugging and abusing 13-year-old Somsack Sinthasomphone in 1988
-Sent to work release at House of Correction in May 1989
-Temporarily moved back to West Allis in March 1990 after his release, then in May moved to his Oxford Apartment in Milwaukee
-From October 1990 to February 1991 committed no known murders for 5 months, although he did try to lure men during this period
-February 1991 lured 17-year-old into his apartment
-April 1991 lured victim Lindsay into his apartment
-May 26, 1991, 14-year-old Konerak Sinthasomphone walked away from Dahmer's apartment into the street, seen by witnesses and reported to Police, who investigated. Explained as a lovers' quarrel. Dahmer then took him back to the apartment and killed him.

-June 30, 1991, traveled to Chicago, attended Pride parade there and lured men from bars
-July 19, back at his apartment
-July 22, Tracy Edwards incident and escape
-Arrested July 22
-Trial January-February 15, 1992 (2 weeks)

I also researched little-known information about Jeffrey's habits, driving routine and vehicles he owned, just to see if there was a red pickup in his history. Additional background information reported that Dahmer never owned a car and always used public transportation. There were suggestions that he did not have a driver's license.

However, the assumption Jeff did not drive appeared incorrect. In Lionel Dahmer's book, he referred to Jeff using his car for job interviews from time to time, and other occasions when "he couldn't drive" only because he was drunk. So, there's history of some driving by Jeff in the late 80's at least, legally, or otherwise.

The most relevant result of this timeline was the fact that Dahmer did in fact move back to his grandmother's house in West Allis early in 1990 after his Corrections release and was in the area when the reported interaction happened: in 1990, when it was cold out. It was reported that the event happened not far from West Allis. If this event happened, according to the timeline it would have most likely been March or early April.

A couple of other stories, again unsubstantiated, once claimed Dahmer was seen in a "nice sports car" trying to pick up a 16-year-old in Northern Illinois. This questionable story was found on social news site Reddit.

Another vehicle-related story was that Dahmer was known to drive a blue van, as he drove them working for a florist's shop in Hollywood, Florida in 1981. A related story had him throwing a boy into the van from a mall, and this story was related to the unproven accusation that he was involved in the Adam Walsh murder, (son of TV personality John Walsh) still attributed to Ottis Toole, partner of serial killer Henry Lee Lucas.

COULD JEFFREY'S DAD BEEN WITH HIM IN INTERACTIONS WITH OTHERS?

This feels like a far-fetched scenario. Lionel Dahmer has been on record attempting to swat away the onslaught of forces that seemed to lead his son into the abyss over the years. At one point he famously encouraged first Jeff's lawyer, then the case judge in 1990 to put Jeffrey into the system as a possible tough love/ scared straight attempt to re-set his course.

The red pickup truck story likely has holes in it somewhere and is not remotely substantiated. Other wild reports of him in different vehicles don't add anything. There was no actual act of trying to approach the people in the street that day, and if any of it is true it would be wild conjecture to assume the older man was Lionel or that the driver was Jeffrey. As sure as the people were that the event happened, it's just as likely the family member and friend were approached by two men, one older, and one who kind of looked like Jeffrey Dahmer, a famous face in the news not long after. Confirmation bias?

Lionel Dahmer was accused of sexually molesting Jeff as a child, a story Jeffrey immediately fervently denied, even by affidavit. This apparently untrue accusation caused Jeffrey's father untold, unnecessary grief. It would be irresponsible to think of the red pickup story any differently, and in any other context without far more actual proof. The reporting party of this incident did not know who Lionel Dahmer was and did not appear aware of Jeffrey's relationship with his dad, nor insinuated the passenger was anyone in particular.

If the driver of the truck was Dahmer, it certainly would be interesting to know the identity of the passenger, though.

REFERENCES

Borowski, John. (2017). *Dahmer's Confession. The Milwaukee Cannibal's arrest statements*. Chicago, IL. Waterfront Productions.

Dahmer, Lionel. (1994). *A Father's Story*. New York, NY. William Morrow.

Davis, D. (1991). *The Milwaukee Murders*. New York, NY. St. Martin's Press.

Dietz, Park E. (1992, February 12). Court testimony at trial of Jeffrey Dahmer. *Court TV*.

Dietz, Park E. (1992a, February 15). Statement in reaction to Dahmer verdict. Letter in Author's possession.

Masters, Brian. (1993). *The Shrine of Jeffrey Dahmer*. London, UK. Hodder & Stoughton.

Touflexis, Anastasia. (1992, February 3). Do mad acts a madman make? *Time*, 17.

Witness: Dahmer said he'd 'eat my heart.' (1992, February 1). *Springfield (IL) State Journal- Register*.

CHAPTER 3

Ed From Plainfield
Just How Crazy was that Guy?

"Q: Last night you also told me about removing Mary's face from her skull. Is that correct or is it not?

A: That's correct."

-from *The Ed Gein File*

Edward Gein. (1957, Milwaukee, USA Harold Olmos/AP/Shutterstock.)

Whenever most people think of the Hitchcock classic, *Psycho*, I assume the shower scene when Norman stabs poor Janet Leigh to death is what comes to mind. And for good reason… it's an iconic, shocking, visceral moment in American horror. In American film, in fact.

Still, my memory of this terrifying story is a different one. My fascination with the study of serial murderers and extreme killers is grounded in the intersection of abnormal psychology and pure horror. When Norman's mother is turned around in her chair to reveal her rotting corpse, dressed and wearing a wig on top of her open-mouthed skull, and the moviegoers come to the realization of the depth of insanity and depravity in which Norman is immersed, that moment stands still in time.

The characters of Norman Bates and his mother were of course, heavily influenced by the very real story out of Plainfield Wisconsin; that of Edward Gein. I've always believed the most terrifying figures are the ones with which you believe you could actually cross paths. Ed Gein's story and his influence on American horror, on more than one occasion, is possibly unmatched.

So, the story of Ed Gein is one that needs to be told and told well. As a person who respects the genre and cares about how it's presented, I'm pleased this story is told by John Borowski, (in his book, *The Ed Gein File*) whose reputation for immersing himself in the history of a subject and "wearing" it, (much like Ed would) is the way it should be done.

The value of such a compilation of documents, interviews, profiles, and the like are difficult to overstate. Anyone who is familiar with the literature of the topic of serial and famous murderers could tell you of the case study and second-hand recounts usually encountered. While there's nothing wrong with most of these resources, the availability of transcripts of actual conversations, rather than someone else's summary and interpretation, is invaluable.

As I pored through the interviews of "Eddie" by investigators and doctors, I was most struck first by the gentle hand they took with him. It's easy to think law enforcement officers and even mental health professionals in 1957 would be less than empathetic with the crazy man who'd murdered a couple of locals and performed bizarre acts of grave robbing and body part collection. When you read these pages and find yourself involved in the conversations, you see the value in the soft, friendly approach and insight that allowed interviewers to ask Ed the most difficult of questions, and elicit, eventually, some rather honest and graphic responses. This was due in no small part by the interviewers' abilities to make Ed feel like they were able to understand what it was like to be there, an empathetic skill difficult to find to this day.

I also was taken by Ed's journey of conversation, from his denials to his "self-serving amnesia or vagueness," as a doctor put it, to his eventual admissions and very clear descriptions of events. Eddie sometimes used wording like "I didn't kill her that I know of," or "I might have done something but not to my knowledge." This verbal qualifying seems to reveal his immaturity, his attempt to obfuscate his responsibility, not as someone who would eventually be found insane by the State of Wisconsin, but by a child who was caught taking money from his mother's purse. Without reading these real-time raw documents, all you remember about Gein is his crazed behavior and being found schizophrenic and legally insane by the doctors who analyzed him and the courts who judged him. Putting yourself in the room where Edward Gein said, "it will show my mental imbalance," gives the reader another view, a context of a man very aware of his status as a person with a mental disturbance and that value as a criminal defense. His continuous references to blackouts and headaches might have been sincere, but the more you read, the more you question.

One last thing I took from those pages is Ed Gein's label as a serial murderer. This was debated by scholars for years because Ed "only" killed 2 victims, Bernice Worden and Mary Hogan. Less so since the FBI adopted the standard of 2 kills to define a serial killer in 2005. He's easily dismissed as an insane grave robber obsessed with his mother's memory. Gein fits with the theory that numbers are irrelevant in determining the serial killer mindset. The fact is, Ed Gein's actions, and his future intent for creating the "dolls" that brought him comfort, is clear by his words and were only ceased by his arrest. Gein was a serial murderer every bit as much as his fellow Wisconsin resident Jeffrey Dahmer and likely would have continued if not detected.

And while I'll always remember and appreciate Gein's influence on films such as Psycho, reading these interviews added a new memory for me: the scene from Silence of the Lambs when Buffalo Bill pranced in front of the mirror, "adjusting" himself to physically appear as a woman... and the admission that Ed Gein had personally preceded this behavior in real life.

Just a bit more graphically.

(Much of this segment was previously published as the Foreword in John Borowski's

2016 book *The Ed Gein File*)

THE BUTCHER OF PLAINFIELD'S INFLUENCE ON POP CULTURE

Ed Gein's crimes, from grave robbing to defiling body parts to serial murder, are highly publicized and well-known.

However, Gein's impact on pop culture just might be one that is unmatched by other serial murderers. While many serial killers these days have a litany of T shirts, books and collectibles, Ed's direct impact on Hollywood just might be without peer. The Butcher of Plainfield was a direct inspiration for horror films such as Alfred Hitchcock's *Psycho*, the academy award winning *Silence of the Lambs* and the *Texas Chainsaw Massacre* franchise.

These are not just horror films. Most consider all of them to be classics and royalty within the nightmare genre.

PSYCHO NORMAN AND ED

Starting with *Psycho*, Ed Gein was the obvious inspiration for the novel by Robert Bloch and resulting film's main character Norman Bates. While Ed did not share Norman's decidedly multiple personality or his taste in women's garments, he did reflect Ed's torturous and unhealthy relationship with his mother.

His repressive household clearly had an emotional and psychological toll on Gein. Ed, born in 1906, was dominated by his fanatical mother and her rantings about religion and the disgusting acts of sex and sin that was committed outside their home. Ed rarely left that home and was not to be exposed to the impure sinners that awaited him. Events at a suspicious fire claimed Ed's older brother Henry's life, a death which always raised questions of Ed's possible involvement.

Ed's obsessive attachment and devotion to his mother ruled his life, as he never dated women or rarely ventured out past the family farm. When she died in 1945, his mental health clearly broke and he kept his mother's room in perfect order, as would a true Norman Bates. While Norman killed those who intruded on his home and business and his existing imaginary relationship with his mother, Ed Gein ventured into the town of Plainfield. He killed and butchered Mary Hogan, a woman who ran a local tavern and Bernice Worden, who ran a hardware store. It's a reasonable question to ask if Gein found two women who were in management or authority positions, running businesses, who reminded him of the image of his domineering mother.

It's also believed that Ed's creation and wearing of a home-made female skin suit was an attempt to re-create his dead mother, not unlike Norman Bates' saving of his mother's corpse while Norman wore her clothes and replicated her actions and speech.

Psycho- 1960. (Parmount/Kobal/Shutterstock.)

A MASSACRE IN TEXAS

The next film commonly credited to Ed Gein's influence is the terrifying 1974 story of the *Texas Chainsaw Massacre*, whose character Leatherface wore a mask of skin and hair removed from a body. Leatherface's character probably contains the fewest actual connections to Ed Gein out of the movies discussed here, other than his interest in utilizing and wearing the face and skin of the dead.

Other details of the film reminiscent of the farm in Plainfield were pieces of furniture at the cannibals' home made from bones and body parts stolen from graveyards, an activity Ed Gein was particularly famous for. Leatherface also appears dressed as a woman at one point, suggesting Norman Bates as well as Gein.

The activities of the cannibal killers of the film and the attacks with chainsaws and other implements were entirely fictional and unrelated to the crimes committed in Wisconsin. The film franchise of *Texas Chainsaw Massacre* continued, however, in multiple remakes and sequels, most recently in February 2022.

Current iteration of the *Chainsaw* franchise co-writer Kim Henkel reportedly "studied" Gein for the film, but also incorporated the personality of Houston serial killer Elmer Wayne Henley. Henley reportedly demonstrated a "conventional morality" in his intent to do the right thing once caught, and Henkel wanted to build this trait into his characters.

DID THE LAMBS STOP SCREAMING?

Ed Gein's last of his trilogy of horror film inspiration was the character of Buffalo Bill in Jonathan Demme's 1991 masterpiece, *Silence of the Lambs*. There were a couple of serial killers in this film, but Gein's most famous activities were found in the Buffalo Bill character, who kidnapped large women, starved them to loosen their skin and "skinned their humps" in order to make a woman's suit.

Ed Gein, along with his penchant for making furniture and articles out of such body parts found from the cemetery swap meet he liked to frequent, did in fact make face masks and body suits of skin to wear as he pranced about his home. Buffalo Bill's supposed pathology included a confusion of gender assignment and a literal DIY transsexual transformation to a woman with the raw materials he stole from his victims.

We do not know how much of Gein's interest in female body suits were directed towards his mother, of personal sexuality, or an effort to "own" a woman of his own, but we know where the idea for Buffalo Bill came from. However, a piece for Crime Libraries written by Katherine Ramsland did state Gein contemplated sex-change surgery so he could become his mother… "to literally crawl into her skin."

To be fair, we cannot give Ed Gein all the credit for *Silence of the Lambs* and Buffalo Bill. Bill's multifaceted psychological makeup is comprised of three well-known serial murderers: Gein, of course, in his use of a skin body suit, Gary Heidnik, who kept his kidnapped women in a basement pit and of course Ted Bundy, who cleverly lured female victims with ruses like wearing a fake cast and feigning helplessness.

SO, WHAT HAPPENED TO ED GEIN'S BROTHER?

Many of Ed Gein's exploits are common knowledge among the serial killer crowd, such as his creations using body parts from the graveyard and his murders that led to his arrest. However, one detail from his early family life is not so commonly known: Ed's older brother Harry died under somewhat mysterious circumstances, and many have come to believe he was Ed Gein's first victim.

Ed and Henry's father, George, died of heart failure on April 1st, 1940. This reportedly was related to his alcoholism, ending his life at 66 years old. Both Henry and Ed worked odd jobs, including handyman work and Ed also babysat. Henry was considered the harder worker of the two. Ed related to the children more easily than he did with his peers.

Peter Vronsky (2004) quoted a neighbor's comments: "Good old Ed. Kind of a loner and maybe a little bit odd with that sense of humor of his, but just the guy to call in and sit with the kiddies when me and the old lady want to go to the show."

On May 16, 1944, Ed reported his brother was missing after they were burning vegetation on the family property. The fire burned out of control at one point and after putting it out, Ed returned to look for Henry. It had become too dark, and Ed assembled a search party. As soon as the party, headed by the local Sheriff arrived, Ed led them straight to where his brother was found face down. They were led to the body by Ed, despite his claim they had been separated by the fire. Initially, it seemed that he was apparently dead due to heart failure. Henry's head was found to have odd multiple bruises while his body showed no injuries from the fire despite being stretched out on a scorched section of ground and his clothes had soot on them. He was also found far from the fire site, so smoke effects appeared unlikely.

Apparently, the death was not suspicious enough for anyone to further investigate. Asphyxiation was listed as the cause of death by the coroner and there was no autopsy. It was thought that Ed, while odd, mentally delayed and childlike, was not capable of committing murder at the time by some.

Not long after Henry's death, Ed's beloved mother Augusta suffered a stroke, resulting in Ed's ascension to the status of her caregiver. Augusta had a second stroke in 1945 and died of related complications in December at age 67. As most people are aware, Ed was destroyed by the death of his mother, and he was left alone desperately mentally ill and unprepared to fend for himself, even as a 39-year-old adult. Ed reacted to her death by boarding up his mother's bedroom and sitting room to be preserved, museum style, as they were when she was alive.

THE DEBATE RAGES

The circumstances at the time of Henry's death were notable. Henry had begun to react to some of his mother's peculiar behaviors and attitudes about women, lack of personal boundaries and other issues. It's possible Harry made comments about the oddly close relationship she and Ed shared. Meanwhile, Ed continued to regard his mother as infallible and placed her firmly on a pedestal. Additionally, Harry had recently begun dating a divorced woman with children. His plan was to soon move in with her. This situation no doubt upset Augusta greatly, who desperately tried to keep the 2 adult brothers at home to keep her remaining family intact. The very thought of him living with a woman at all, let alone in a sinful relationship would have driven Augusta wild. It's very likely this was a volatile source of angst and conflict between Ed and Harry, with the latter now freely speaking of his mother with disrespect and with Ed reacting in anger.

According to Harold Schechter in his book, *Deviant*, Eddie was "astonished" that Henry appeared to have serious questions about Augusta and her hold over Ed. Eddie had always believed that Henry shared his own view of his mother, "regarding her as infallible, faultless, a saint on Earth. Henry's implied criticism of Augusta came as a real shock to Eddie. It was something he just couldn't understand. And it was something he would never forget."

This is the main reason it's easy for people to speculate that Ed somehow killed his brother in an emotional reaction to Harry's behavior and plans. Later, investigators and researchers have come to believe that Harry was in fact Ed Gein's first victim, particularly in light of his final horrific activities of graverobbing and murder.

Of course, speculation was easy. Some wondered aloud if Ed's mother had something to do with Harry's death, pressing Ed like Anthony Perkins in *Psycho*. And the fire… was it arson? A diversion or attempt at a coverup? Details of the fire were widely debated… that it was accidental; that it was Eddie's idea. Ed insisted that it was Henry's.

Schechter quoted Ed Gein when questioned about the suspicious fact that he'd led searchers directly to Henry's body despite being unable to locate him earlier: "Funny how that works."

Others felt the action of murdering Harry looked nothing like his murders of Warden and Hogan. But if Ed's mental capacity was a true factor in his murderous behaviors, an emotional reaction in the case of Harry would easily be as understandable as his bizarre murders and post-mortem mutilations of the 2 women years later. Ed would certainly be considered a disorganized offender, complete with a believable variance in victimology and behaviors.

More disputes in theory would claim that Ed seemed to "snap" after his mother's death, not before. And that his interest in bodies and death were consistent in his past behaviors, but not the homicide of a sibling. This is still rebutted by the very possible act of Ed defending his mother's saintly honor, and possibly following her wishes. Ed's later murders were described by Ed as committed during period of mental "dazes." If Ed wasn't directed to commit murder by his mother, could he have entered into a murderous "daze" after a conflict with his brother who dared to impugn her character?

REFERENCES

Borowski, John. (2016). *The Ed Gein File*. A psycho's confession and case documents. Chicago, IL. Waterfront Productions.

Dressler, Jacob. (2020, July 22). Iconic horror movies that were inspired by serial killer Ed Gein. *ScreenGeek*. www.screengeek.net.

Heinitz, Lexi. (2021, July 20). The three iconic horror films inspired by serial killer Ed Gein. *Looper*. www.looper.com.

Lerner, Jamie. (2021, April 9). Deranged killer Ed Gein's first victim might have been his brother. *Distractify*. www.disractify.com.

Psycho. (1960). Shamley Productions. Paramount Pictures.

Ramsland, Katherine. (2013, December 2). The ultimate ghoul. *Crimelibrary. Criminal*

Minds & methods. www.trutv.com.

Schechter, Harold. (1998). *Deviant: The shocking true story of Ed Gein, the original "Psycho."* New York, NY. Gallery Books.

Silence of the Lambs. (1991). Strong Heart Productions. Orion Pictures.

The Texas Chainsaw Massacre. (1974). Vortex. Bryanston Distributing.

Thomas, Leah. (2022, February 18). The true story behind 'Texas Chainsaw Massacre' is even creepier than you think. *Cosmopolitan*. https://sports.yahoo.com.

Vronsky, Peter. (2004). *Serial killers: The method and madness of monsters*. New York, NY. Berkley Publishing/Penguin.

CHAPTER 4

Headed to Disneyland.
From the Walk-in Killer to the Night Stalker.

"I would shoot them in the head and they would wiggle and squirm all over the place and then just stop; or cut them with a knife and watch their face turn real white."

-Richard Ramirez

Richard Ramirez. (Los Angeles, USA AP/Shutterstock.)

Richard Ramirez. The "Night Stalker." One of the classic, iconic names in serial murder lore, was dead. An ignominious end after over two and a half decades in a prison cell at age 53. At the end, Ramirez remained readily recognizable, and still had his shock of long black hair. He did not provide a gradual, visual graying fade like another member of his California brethren of death, Charles Manson. He was still a recognizable face, although with a pretty set of brand-new teeth, courtesy of the State of California. The basic preservation of this image could serve to cement his historical status... a serial killer Elvis, if you will.

THE PASSING OF RICHARD RAMIREZ

Ramirez died on June 7, 2013, at Marin General Hospital in Greenbrae, California of complications secondary to B-cell lymphoma. At the time of his death Ramirez had other significant conditions, including "chronic substance abuse and chronic hepatitis C viral infection," according to the coroner's report. Ramirez had been on death row for more than 23 years, still pursuing appeals while awaiting execution by the state of California.

Alan Yochelson, who prosecuted Ramirez, said that although the state did not execute Ramirez, "some measure of justice has been achieved" because he had to live out his life behind bars.

Is that true?

Did half a life on Death Row pay for the spectacular murders committed by Ramirez?

Is that what people think?

Ramirez' story is not a new one. He committed a rampage of violent assaults, home invasions and killings from June 1984 to August 1985 that paralyzed the Los Angeles area... causing citizens to block their doors at night and not take out the garbage after dark. Movie theatres grew empty while sales of home alarms and handguns spiked. His crimes also cast the region under a national spotlight.

His assaults were gruesome. Originally dubbed the "Walk-in Killer" for his brazen home invasions, he was eventually nicknamed the "Night Stalker" as he attacked most of his victims after invading their homes at night. He cut out the eyes of one victim, left Devil-worshipping pentagrams at the crime scene of another, and raped and murdered women after shooting the men they were with.

It's believed he killed at least 14 people, ranging from age 9 to 83. He beat 2 elderly women to death with a hammer. He sexually assaulted children. He drew signs and slogans like "Jack the Knife" at scenes. He committed countless violent sexual assaults and killed by bludgeoning, knife attacks and shooting. He electrocuted one victim. He forced a female victim to swear her love for Satan.

After his conviction and death sentence, he famously quipped, "I'll see you in Disneyland."

Night Stalker Investigators, San Francisco, USA. (Jeff Reinking/AP/Shutterstock)

Responses to Ramirez' death were varied.

One of his final attack victims, Bill Carns, told TMZ the death was a "reason to celebrate" and that he was headed out for a Mexican feast. He said, "I feel better already... I feel like I lost 50 pounds, like a huge weight has been lifted off of [sic] my shoulders... Saying that I'm happy he's dead is too simple."

Shelly Ramirez, niece of the deceased killer, said after the death, "I felt free. What he did was sick. I'm sorry about what happened to the families."

Ms. Ramirez recounted an incident when during a visit at San Quentin he masturbated in front of her. He said he would "fuck her any day" if she wasn't his niece. He became angry during the same visit because she was wearing a gold necklace with a cross, declaring "Satanists don't wear gold."

Ramirez apparently had a habit of masturbating in front of staff, young girls, and others. An official stated there were several incidents of exposure at the prison and sexual acts in front of others. His personal visits were curtailed in 2004 after masturbating in front of a young girl, and again in 2007 for a similar offense. He reportedly did not have much visitation after that; none in 2010 and towards the end had refused to visit with anyone.

WAS A MEASURE OF JUSTICE ACHIEVED?

Still, it's difficult to think that the Night Stalker's sentence of a life behind bars was justice for the victims and their families. A sentence of death made for a great headline, but it was always unlikely a death sentence would be administered given the politics of California. And if you asked Richard, I imagine he would have enjoyed the stardom of an execution far more than the quiet death of cancer that eventually claimed him.

The scrawny kid from a terrible background with rotting teeth and breath so foul people would turn their heads, still managed to live the life of a celebrity, one many people in this fame-fueled world would take in a heartbeat, thank you.

Ramirez received bags full of mail over 20 years after entering San Quentin's death row and more than 15 years after marrying wife Doreen, who wrote him 75 letters. The demand for visitation requests never waned.

The constant correspondence and requests for artwork, which Ramirez often happily obliged, never slowed. Online murderabilia related to Ramirez was and is always in demand.

Here's a piece of signed art I obtained at one point by Ramirez:

Art by Richard Ramirez. (Author photo.)

Something a high-school kid might doodle in bright-colored markers on the back of a science notebook. But in this case, an artifact worthy of value, from a star?

While his acts were positively repulsive, Ramirez' dark brooding looks and California notoriety made him a star during his trial, and he relished every moment of it. Many people: kids, women admirers and even some men will always revel in the allure of a counter-culture icon and the fame that accompanies him. It's understandable why the sunglasses-adorned rock star killer gained so much attention in 1989.

But his death was in 2013. You could still buy a Richard Ramirez T-shirt very quickly and easily – even before his death. As you can to this day.

Night Stalker song lyrics are still found on the Internet in an instant.

On tumblr, a site named "Bitches love Ramirez" revealed a rabid fandom by girls and kids born years after The Night Stalker was busy raping and murdering women in California.

And around the time of his death, rumors circulated that Hollywood Star James Franco agreed to star and direct a movie about Ramirez' life. Years later, actor Lou Diamond Phillips was reported to have signed on to star as the Night Stalker as well. And who could forget the popular, campy depictions of Ramirez in the TV hit *American Horror Story?*

Not too shabby an ending to a script that started out pretty badly.

"A measure of justice achieved?"

What do you think?

(Parts of this article were originally printed in *Serial Killer Magazine* in 2013, not long after Ramirez' death.)

CREATING A SERIAL KILLER

As a teacher of Serial Murder, deciding on the order of things… classes, presentations, film, discussions, to me, is a challenging strategy. It always seemed important how you build your classes regarding base information, then adding to that, and saving items that require a higher element of understanding or include what could be considered a cumulative example of knowledge acquired over the course of the semester, for the conclusion.

It didn't take me long to decide that the case study of Richard Ramirez really is the ideal case to discuss on the last night of class. His differences from other serial killers were always notable, in his wildly varied methods of killing as well as his inconsistent victimology. It seemed the only thing important to Ramirez was that killed someone… regardless of how, or whom.

As well, I've always considered Ramirez as that killer who ticks all the boxes on a chart of potential factors in the creation of a serial killer. Ramirez defied the usual convention of nature vs. nurture. He was more like "all of the above."

During the semester we talk about many variables. One is biological disposition. In the 70s, we did not have the luxury of the sophisticated brain scans, brain structure examination and genetic analysis that are used today with potential psychopaths and violent offenders. However, anecdotal and confirmed reports of Ramirez tells that story.

"Richie," as a child, appeared to suffer from temporal lobe epilepsy. He may or may not have shared this with serial killer John Wayne Gacy, whose fainting spells sometimes seemed more convenient than organic. But Richie did in fact suffer from this malady, resulting in grand mal seizures in school. As well as disrupting his physiology, it left him with an inability to play football or participate in other games with his friends, which contributed to his developing antisocial behavior, alienation, anger, and isolation.

While on the subject of biology, consider that Ramirez' mother toiled long hours in the Tony Lamais boot factory, inhaling what was believed to be toxic fumes from mixing chemicals like benzene, xylene and toluene with little protection in the late 1950s. This inhalation was thought to result in birth defects, which was the case while she was pregnant with Ramirez. Richie's brother suffered from physical defects since birth. Other siblings did as well. It's also been suggested that bomb testing at the time in nearby New Mexico, carried infectants to food and drink. This as well as Richie's mother's prenatal conditions could have contributed to all of the children's birth defects.

Ramirez was violently beaten by his father, potentially resulting in head or brain injuries. This was also an early lesson in the technique of violence to gain control. He also reportedly suffered multiple head injuries from being knocked out by a swing at age five, which preceded his epileptic seizures, and at two a dresser fell on his head.

Ramirez' father's violence and sudden, erratic behavior was also exhibited in his beating himself in the head with a hammer, modelling bizarre violence to Richard and possibly suggesting a trait he may have passed down to his son.

Finally, a serious biological factor could also have been his drug addiction and alcohol abuse. Richard took to cannabis abuse as early as age 10 and then sniffing glue, taking LSD, and moved on to cocaine and more as he got older.

Moving onto environmental factors, Ramirez added to his long list of developmental influences when he was reportedly sexually abused in his home. There was supposedly a child molester who had been hired to tutor Richard's brother and it's unlikely Richard escaped his advances, although he did not acknowledge this occurring. I wonder if some things are too disturbing to admit, even by the Night Stalker.

Reports also include his father tying him to a cross in the graveyard as punishment, fueling more anger, terror, and hatred for religion.

Ramirez had the terrible misfortune of being close to a cousin who returned from the Vietnam War psychologically scarred. The cousin, Miguel ("Mike") showed Richard horrifying graphic photos of violent atrocities against women the cousin participated in while overseas, and at 12, Richard was enthralled by the gore. Photos and stories of severed heads, rape and murder filled Ramirez' still-developing psyche at an age when a boy was most susceptible to influence. Mike was a terrible influence on Richard, promoting and encouraging violence, particularly against women, criminal behavior, and drug use. Richard later admitted to sexual arousal by the photos of the rape/murder victims shown to him by Mike.

Mike displayed the worst kind of modelling to Richard, who was in a formative stage in his life and was fusing sex with violence. Mike, after an argument with his wife, shot her in the face and killed her in front of Ramirez. The visceral experience of this graphic violence couldn't possibly have affected Ramirez in any way other than push him towards violence, a path it seemed for which he was destined. He stated he never admitted he saw the murder at the time at the direction of his cousin. It remains to be seen if he could have received some sort of psychological help that could have put him on a detour from the Highway to Hell on which he was travelling.

Incredibly, Mike was released from an insane asylum despite the murder of his wife and picked up where he left off with Richard, sharing fantasies of murder and violence against women while high on drugs. This was undeniably adding fuel to the fire that was to erupt soon.

Finally, Richard's involvement in Satan worshipping, in my view, sealed his deal with the Devil.

Richard's eventual turn towards Satanism could have been a direct rejection of the strong Catholic upbringing he was exposed to as a child. Richard was known to sleep in a cemetery after prowling the streets at night as a boy, peeping in windows and practicing his nocturnal activities that culminated in the creation of the Night Stalker. Ramirez was exposed to these activities after moving in with an uncle who was an "obsessive peeping Tom." He was also known to pray to Satan while resting in the garden of the dead that he chose as a peaceful place to sleep.

Another event which must be considered significant was, as a teen, he was working in a hotel and attempted to rape a woman in her room. Her husband returned and caught Ramirez in the act. The couple, from out of town did not want to return for trial so charges were dropped. Richard had gotten away with attempted rape, and this helped convince him that he was protected by Satan himself, a belief he carried while committing his reign of terror, laughing at the public and authorities along the way.

If there were ever a killer who was a culmination of a semester's worth of potential serial murder developmental facts and various elements within the biological and environmental, it was Richard Ramirez.

Richard Ramirez. (Los Angeles, USA Nick Ut/AP/Shutterstock.)

WAS RAMIREZ PROTECTED BY SATAN?

One topic that's unexplored in Ramirez' story is the feeling he had that he was protected by Satan while committing his crimes. Clearly his strong Catholic family background led to a level of rebellion and rejection by Richie, but as each example was presented to him by the mysterious unknown, dark forces seemed to help him along his way down the path of multiple murders and sexual assaults.

I have to start with the aforementioned 1977 report of Ramirez' sexual assault, when at approximately age 15, while working at a Holiday Inn. Supposedly Ramirez got into the habit of stealing from patrons and peeping on women in their rooms. It's also reported that he fondled and molested two children in an elevator but was not prosecuted. At one point, the Young Night Stalker decided he'd found a woman alone, available, and vulnerable enough for the fledgling serial rapist to collect. His attack was clumsy and unsuccessful, as he did not plan on the woman's husband returning to the room while he was in the act.

Reportedly the husband beat Ramirez very badly. Unfortunately for the Los Angeles area, he wasn't incapacitated by the attack by the furious husband. However, even more unfortunately for all of Ramirez' future victims, the couple decided they did not want to travel back to Texas for the prosecution, testimony and trial and Richard Ramirez had been given his first free pass by the dark forces that guided him. This was Ramirez' first indication he was being protected by a higher, sinister power.

After his killing career was underway, in March 1985 he'd entered the home of Vincent and Maxine Zazzara. He shot Mr. Zazzara in the head while he slept and while his attention was diverted looking for valuables, Mrs. Zazzara picked up the shotgun the couple kept under the bed and levelled it at Ramirez. She pulled the trigger, only to have her heart sink as the click of an empty chamber was all that resulted. This was another moment when Richard Ramirez' reign of terror should have ended. It would later be revealed that Mr. Zazzara had unloaded the shotgun in anticipation of grandchildren visiting the house that weekend. A thoughtful act of safety and care for the children caused their method of self-defense to let her down at the worst possible moment. Instead, an enraged Ramirez shot Mrs. Zazzara three times, grabbed a knife from the kitchen and according to Philip Carlo's *Night Stalker*, unsuccessfully attempted to cut her heart out. He then furiously tore her eyes out for daring to end the Night Stalker. The ferocity of the mutilation he displayed in his twisted anger for a person threatening him was remarkable. It's also believed that the presence of Maxine's Bibles in the house had further infuriated the Devil worshipper. Again, after facing the pulled trigger of a shotgun aimed at his head, it had been proven to Richard that he was under the protection of a dark angel.

Ramirez continued his belief that he was protected by Satan. After one kidnapping attempt, he committed a traffic violation in a stolen car. How many Joel Rifkins and Ted

Bundys were pulled over and arrested after a traffic stop? But when Ramirez was pulled over, he fortuitously overheard the broadcast reporting a kidnapping on the officer's radio. He managed to run away, but not before he drew a pentagram on the car's hood to remind everyone with whom they were dealing.

Within the stolen car, a business card for a dentist was found. Investigation revealed a man named Richard Mena, matching Ramirez' description had been in for X-rays. Wisely tracking Richard's possible dentist to handle his rotting, painful teeth, Police officers were staged in position waiting for his arrival. After time passed, they installed an alarm for employees to trigger when the killer returned. They did. The alarm that was sounded never went off. At this point Detective Gil Carrillo said, "how many more people are going to die?"

And finally, after Ramirez committed a murder in the Bay area, San Francisco Mayor Dianne Feinstein decided to completely blow the entire investigation up to that point by announcing the critical accumulated information that had been kept out of the public's knowledge at a press conference for all to hear. Feinstein revealed the caliber of the gun and even more crucially, the fact he'd left footprints with his distinctive shoes. Ramirez couldn't drop the incriminating size 11.5 Avia athletic shoes into the Bay fast enough. Satan had smiled on him one more time.

Ramirez was finally identified through dogged and determined investigative work and ultimately caught by a mob who beat and detained him for Police, and the disciple of the Prince of Darkness was finally in custody, for good. During the trial, Ramirez rejected any suggestions he might be insane; he wanted to instead proclaim his allegiance to Satan. The son of the Zazzara couple, Peter Zazzara, remarked that "Ramirez had a Satanic hold over the case and the courtroom."

Given the number of lives lost after repeated incredible twists of fortune that fell Ramirez' way understandably fueled his brazen rampage and drug-assisted belief that he was a soldier for Satan himself. And anyone who believes in Christianity could rightfully suspect this could be true.

REFERENCES

Biography: Richard Ramirez: The Night Stalker. (2004). A & E Home Video.

Blankstein, Andrew & Mather, Kate. (2013, June 7). 'Night Stalker' prosecutor says Ramirez death ends 'tragic period.' *Los Angeles Times*. www.latimes.com.

Carlo, Phillip. (1996). *The Night Stalker: The life and crimes of Richard Ramirez*. New York, NY. Pinacle Books, Kensington Publishing Group.

Giannangelo, Stephen J. (2013). Some measure of justice achieved? The passing of Richard Ramirez. *Serial Killer Magazine*, Issue 14.

McMahon, James. (2011, January 20). James Franco to play serial killer Richard Ramirez in 'The Night Stalker.' *NME*. www.nme.com.

N'Duka, Amanda. (2015, June 10). 'Night Stalker' Movie: Lou Diamond Phillips to play L. A. serial killer Richard Ramirez. *Deadline*. https//deadline.com.

Parry, Emma & Diaz, Alex. (2021, January 23). Son of Night Stalker Richard Ramirez victims says, 'I wish I'd blown his f***ing head off' in wake of Netflix show. *The U.S. Sun*. www.the-sun.com.

Pelisek, Christine. (2019, October 22). My uncle the serial killer: Night Stalker Richard Ramirez's niece on his death. *Daily Beast*. www.thedailybeast.com.

TMZ. (2013, June 7). Night Stalker attack victim- I'm thrilled he's dead. *www.TMZ.com*.

Verhoeven, Bernice. (2021, January 16). 'Night Stalker': 10 most terrifying details about 'satanic' serial killer Richard Ramirez. *The Wrap*. www.thewrap.com.

CHAPTER 5

Kuklinski and Kaczynski; The Iceman and The Unabomber. Serial Killers or Something Else?

"Assassin? That sounds so exotic. I was just a murderer."
-Richard Kuklinski

In a later chapter, I take on some of the elements that define serial murder. However, here, I look at a couple of offenders that for the longest time, were never really considered serial killers, because they had a different title. The "Iceman," mob hitman Richard Kuklinski and the "Unabomber," domestic terrorist Ted Kaczynski.

A hitman has traditionally not been included in a grouping of serial murderers as they seemed to have a purpose, that they were simply paid assassins or just conducting business. The idea was that if they weren't getting paid, they wouldn't be killing anyone. Few people would consider Tony Soprano a serial killer if you asked them on the street. Even hitmen are insulted by the suggestion they were serial killers. In an interview, mob contract killer Donald "Tony the Greek" Frankos scoffed at the idea of being a serial killer. The admitted murderer of at least 40 men sneered at the label of the serial killer, who "preys on weak people… gets his joys" and commits "perverted acts and kills them."

As well, a terrorist has been traditionally considered a killer with a purpose as well, whether they believe their acts are altruistic, for the greater good, a religious motivation or a misguided principle.

Today, researchers often simply consider anyone who kills multiple people in different events for any reason to be serial killers, without real consideration of psychological motivation. But Kuklinski, I think, forced a challenge to prior assumptions not just because he killed multiple people, but why.

Kuklinski demonstrated that he truly enjoyed killing people, elevating it to an art form, really.   Convicted of murdering 6 people but claiming to have killed hundreds more, he took a pride and apparent enjoyment in his craft that really does transcend the garden-variety Mafia hitman doing his job. Besides, Kuklinski didn't just kill on assignment; he killed ostensibly for his own reasons as well, business or otherwise.

This is a killer who shared the oft-cited psychopathic history of torturing and killing neighborhood cats and dogs, demonstrating a sadism and enjoyment for inflicting harm that's usually reserved for those who can play at destroying what regular people consider pets.

At age 13 he beat a town bully to death. Later, he grew into an Ed Kemper physical type of imposing figure at 6' 5" and nearly 300 pounds. Seems Kuklinski could have been yet another argument for the on again off again theory of XYY violence.

It's fair to say that this was a psychopath who found the perfect career choice as opposed to a sociopath who was molded by his surroundings and unfortunate trauma like a Tony Soprano character.

It's said he killed often just for fun, at random, or while looking for the slightest provocation. His methods and victim selection were so varied it confounded authorities; his research and professional outlook on his craft made him the perfect nightmare. A description of Kuklinski by other criminals, who looked at him as something beyond anything they had considered before, was "the devil himself."

In a 2017 interview for *Real Crime* magazine, I answered a number of editorial and reporting staff questions. Many of my comments made it into the final article, but I think a presentation of the conversation in its entirety is worth reading. The entire exchange follows:

Do you have to be a psycho to be a hitman?

I don't know that a mental disorder is absolutely necessary. I'd compare that to gang activity of today, where many kids are a product of their environments, where poverty and powerlessness is a breeding ground for extreme measures to escape such a life. The rewards that can come with gang activity, or in Kuklinski's heyday Organized Crime life, can be voluminous: money, status, power, women. It's not hard to see how some people could eventually justify that this life is forced on them, that it's their only way to survive or succeed, and that they are convinced their circumstances are not their fault.

Richard Kuklinski. (1986, Hackensack, USA Mike Derer/AP/Shutterstock.)

What kind of mind does it take and what toll does killing for profit have on the mind?

It depends on the individual. A person I described as a product of their environment can compartmentalize and justify their actions. They can be narcissistic and immature and believe their own excuses. It is possible they could reflect on the damage to peoples' lives. A psychopath or a sociopath, however, could adapt, even thrive in this life with little difficulty and no distress to their sensibilities. There's still a narcissism and a disdain for those who live a lawful life consistent with that personality that is compatible with murder for hire. In these cases, I see no toll on that sort of mind.

It seems Kuklinski's enjoyment in being interviewed and appearing in the media exemplifies a love for the fame and status reflective of his mindset, not unlike some high-profile serial killers.

What makes a cold-blooded killer tick?

I think the type most often described as "cold-blooded" is a psychopathic or sociopathic personality, someone who has no remorse, no feelings, guilt, empathy, or any aversion to violence. These people, like Kuklinski, have often had violence in their childhoods so extreme that it's normal, and is the only way they know how to deal with anything. This makes them more equipped for the job as a hitman. However, the predatory nature of a psychopath... the "cold-bloodedness" you describe... acts in concert with a certain amount of patience and manipulativeness, and often intelligence, that makes them good at what they do. A successful hitman is someone who can do it for 30 years like a Kuklinski, rather than someone caught in the early stages of their careers.

I think Kuklinski is one of the few hitmen that I would say crossed over into the realm of a full-blown serial killer. Researchers and FBI nowadays include many multiple murder offenders in their statistics as serial murderers without much regard for motivation. But some, mainly those more oriented towards the psychological angle of study, still look at serial killers as those who kill for a reason, a psychological "need." Kuklinski continued to kill for far more reasons than a guy who was paid well and lived the good life; he killed because he loved it.

The Iceman kept saying "I didn't feel nothing" when the interviewer asked him how he felt during the murders. Did he really feel nothing or was he just refusing to feel?

Regarding feeling "nothing..." he simply didn't feel anything. Ted Bundy and Jeffrey Dahmer needed alcohol to commit many of their murders. Kuklinski had no such inhibitions to overcome. He enthusiastically tortured animals as a child... and as found significant by researchers of human to animal violence, he enjoyed torture of animals normally regarded as "pets" (dogs and cats) indicating a non-empathetic, sadistic, impulse-driven need for violence that precludes any "feelings" to disregard.

Kuklinski was a full-blown psychopath... actually, more accurately a sociopath if we are to believe he was just a product of a horrific upbringing of poverty, violence, and abuse. A child living in a household of violence normalizes it and even thrives in it. Of course, without testing, we will not know what Kuklinski's genetics might be, or if there were other biological factors regarding his development.

How hard is it to maintain the dual facade that the Iceman was living? On one hand a suburban family man on the other a Mafia hitman?

Some people could say that Kuklinski exhibited "doubling," a psychological process where an individual can live 2 entirely different and seemingly conflicting lives separate from one another. This was a theory made popular by Robert Lifton regarding Nazi-era doctors. But Kuklinski, in my opinion, simply was participating in the compartmentalized parts of his life. His position as a vicious, high status, feared hitman who was able to enjoy the violence, success and respect his business brought him was one major part of his life. The other part was his home life, where he could be the loving and protective father, who also exhibited power, violence, and control. He needed to extend the intelligence he exhibited in avoiding law enforcement in the meticulous manner he did for as long as he did. I can't imagine the duplicity was all that difficult for him.

This sort of dual life isn't particularly unheard of with a psychopathic serial murderer. Dennis Rader, the BTK Killer, had no issues living a similar double life as a killer and a family man.

Kuklinski talked about 'moving heaven and earth' to kill someone who made him angry and was especially protective of his wife and kids. Was this pride talking, protecting his reputation, or did he genuinely care about his family?

I'd say all the above. A prototypical sociopath is going to be highly defensive of his status, how he is perceived, almost to the point of paranoia. This drives a lot of his pathological need for control. He was known for an extreme aversion for public embarrassment and any hint of disrespect. The defense of his family is partially because he cares for them but is just as much driven by how he is viewed, and how anyone could dare threaten someone in his circle.

It should be noted that Kuklinski did seem to have a genuine concern for the effect of the exposure of his criminal life had on his family, not unlike the BTK Killer and Albert DeSalvo, among others. So, a concern for his family isn't completely surprising.

A SERIAL MURDERER IS ARRESTED WHILE DISPLAYING HIS SKILL

Richard Kuklinski was arrested at a New Jersey Turnpike rest stop, apprehended by undercover BATF agents during "Operation Iceman," named for Richard's moniker earned by reportedly freezing some of his victims.

Kuklinski was found to have shown undercover Agent Dominick Polifrone his technique for poisoning a person with cyanide. He was taped describing cyanide as an efficient murder weapon, saying, "it's quiet, it's not messy, it's not noisy… you can spray it in someone's face and they go to sleep." These tapes also included his admitting to past and planned murders, and asking where he could get more cyanide, which sealed his murder convictions.

The Iceman admitted after a plea he killed George Malliband, who Kuklinski said was shot over "business" in 1980. It was later reported Malliband came to Kuklinski's home to conduct business, which Kuklinski strongly objected to. Malliband then threatened Richard's family, a fatal choice. He also admitted after a plea to killing pharmacist Paul Hoffman, who wanted Kuklinski to supply him with stolen ulcer drugs (Tagamet) in 1982. Louis Masgay, Kuklinski's partner, was shot in the head after meeting Kuklinski with $95,000 for stolen videocassette recorder tapes. He was frozen for 2 years before being dumped in 1983. In 1982 and 1983, Kuklinski, frustrated by what he considered to be the bumbling efforts of his 2 co-operatives in a stolen car ring, killed both Gary Smith and Dan Deppner. Smith was murdered by Kuklinski and Deppner with a poisoned hamburger and strangled, then Deppner was later killed with cyanide poison.

Kuklinski was convicted and sentenced to life in 1988. In 2003, he received an additional 30 years' sentence after confessing to the murder of a Police officer who was associated with the mob.

A MURDERER PASSES

Kuklinski died in the prison wing of St. Francis Hospital in Trenton, New Jersey in March 2006 at the age of 70.

He was known for promoting his notoriety by appearing in HBO documentaries as well as meeting with criminologists, writers, and psychiatrists. He occasionally took the publicity tour too far as with his stories about his role in the Jimmy Hoffa murder or his supposed storing of a corpse in the freezer of a Mr. Softee ice cream truck for 2 years. Other claims, including that he killed Roy DeMeo, a Gambino crime family member, were also disputed.

In his documentaries, the former altar boy stated he'd killed between 100-200 people and first disclosed his murder of an NYPD detective in 1980. In another, his wife described their cushy suburban life as "The all-American family." However, one book quoted Mrs. Kuklinski of claiming her husband once tried to smother her with a pillow, tried to run her over with a car and broke her nose 3 times.

Barbara Kuklinski also told various outlets that she married Kuklinski out of fear, after he'd stabbed her in the chest once and later threatened to kill her mother if she didn't marry him.

She described him as "a raging psychopath" who would "constantly abuse me, slashing me, throwing things at me." She said, "with Richard, it wasn't so much rage. It was control."

She also said, "but he loved me. I have no doubt about that."

THE UNABOMBER IS HEARD FROM

Meanwhile, in 2016, I noticed a report that Ted Kaczynski, the famous Unabomber, was in the news after a long period of hibernation. A CBS News report recounted how Kaczynski sent a hand-written letter to a writer from *The New Yorker* named Lawrence Wright according to CBS News Correspondent Anna Werner. Reportedly, it had been sent to other journalists. The letter contained new attacks on his brother, who helped end the Unabomber saga.

Ted Kaczynski wrote in his letter that he was "ready to speak to someone from the media regarding my brother's recent comments and to discuss how they are being used to torment me." He also listed guidelines, including "1. tell me who you are," "2. why I should trust you" and to acknowledge "that you understand that I am NOT mentally ill as my brother, Dave, would have you believe."

This letter, of course, was broadcast everywhere. Always ready for another interview, I kind of took this as an invitation. While I wasn't a member of the media, I took it on myself to write Mr. Kaczynski, politely introduce myself and suggest an unknown educator such as me could be an interesting person to use as an outlet for his comments. I was, disappointingly, unsuccessful.

Ted Kaczynski. (Helena, USA. Douglas C. Pizac/AP/Shutterstock.)

Ted did in fact write me back and politely denied that he was sending out letters as reported, at all. He also told me in no uncertain terms he didn't want to talk about anything else, either.

AN UNEXPLAINED MOVE

In December 2021, Kaczynski was transferred to a prison medical facility in North Carolina, from the Supermax in Florence, Colorado. A statement from the Federal Bureau of Prisons (BOP) announced that "Theodore John Kaczynski is in the custody of the Federal Bureau of Prisons at the Federal Medical Center (FMC) Butner." The statement continued with spokesman Donald Murphy stating, "for safety and security reasons, we do not discuss the specific conditions of an inmate's confinement, to include medical information or reasons for transfer/redesignation."

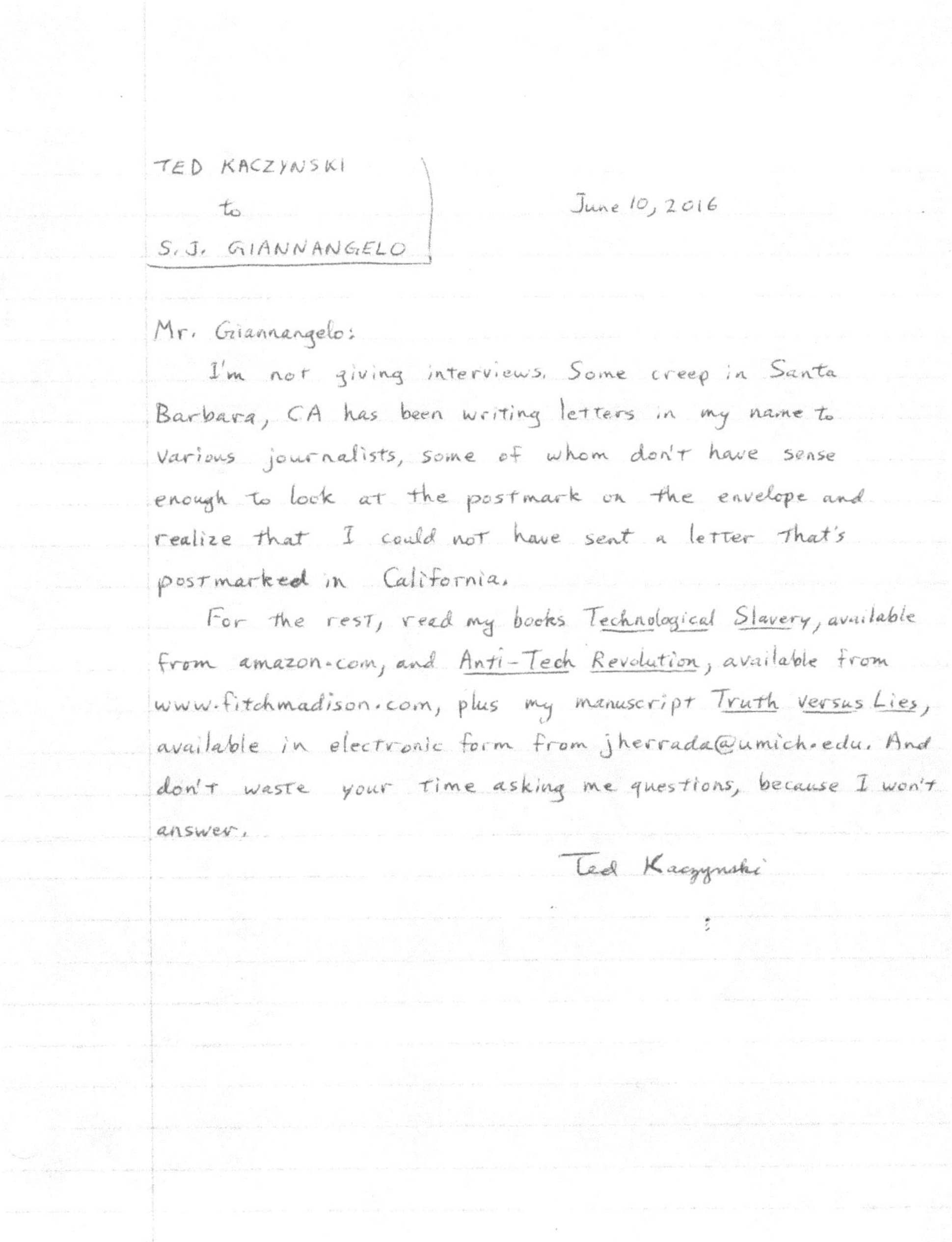

TED KACZYNSKI
to
S. J. GIANNANGELO

June 10, 2016

Mr. Giannangelo:

    I'm not giving interviews. Some creep in Santa Barbara, CA has been writing letters in my name to various journalists, some of whom don't have sense enough to look at the postmark on the envelope and realize that I could not have sent a letter that's postmarked in California.

    For the rest, read my books Technological Slavery, available from amazon.com, and Anti-Tech Revolution, available from www.fitchmadison.com, plus my manuscript Truth versus Lies, available in electronic form from jherrada@umich.edu. And don't waste your time asking me questions, because I won't answer.

                        Ted Kaczynski

(photo by Author)

Kaczynski spent previous decades in the maximum-security federal prison for his convictions for murdering 3 people within a series of 16 targeted bombings towards scientists and other identified individuals and symbolic targets like universities and airlines (the source of the "una" part of his nickname). The Unabomber also injured 23 other people in various locations of the country between 1978 and 1995. He was arrested at a remoted cabin in Western Montana in 1996 after assistance from his brother, who recognized Kaczynski's writings.

Kaczynski's murders included an advertising executive, a computer rental store owner and a timber industry lobbyist. He maimed a Yale University computer expert and a California geneticist. The Harvard graduate strongly rejected any sort of insanity defense and stated in his journals that his motive was "simply personal revenge."

Ted Kaczynski's brother's tip led authorities to Ted's tiny Montana cabin which contained "a mountain of evidence" including bomb parts, journal entries describing the targets and handwritten drafts of his manifesto. One completed bomb was ready for mailing to another victim. Many of these items were sold at a 2011 auction in Atlanta which generated approximately $190,000 for victims and family members.

Ted was arraigned in California and New Jersey, the locations of the 3 fatal bombings and he pleaded guilty in exchange for a sentence of life in prison without the possibility of parole in January 1998.

Unabomber Auction. (Atlanta, USA David Goldman/AP/Shutterstock.)

FMC Butner offers medical services for prisoners including oncology, surgery, neuro-diagnostics, and dialysis according to the BOP. They house 771 inmates and has hosted such names as Bernie Madoff, who died there in 2021, and John Hinckley Jr.

A SERIAL KILLER OR ...?

Like The Iceman, The Unabomber is another one who people might debate regarding whether he's a serial killer, a terrorist, a murderer, a political activist, or something else.

Kaczynski killed three people during his reign of terror over 2 decades and by luck alone could have killed many more instead of just injuring them. Researchers these days would simply call him a serial killer because of his multiple murders in separate events. Very few serial killers, outside of Richard Chase and a handful of others, could be considered insane by the legal system, but Ted, despite his protestations, is right there. Still, is he different than Herbert Mullin? Just because his reported mental illness looks like a simple enhanced paranoia rather than full-blown delusions, is it different? The fact is Mullin and Chase are without question serial killers, as Kaczynski should be, and if his intent was more successful, he could have a much more impressive list of kills.

He's still very responsible for his actions, obviously displaying a callous disregard for human life as it intersects with his political beliefs, and like Anders Breivik and Dylan Roof, vehemently denies any mental illness affecting his mind's processes and decisions. On paper, according to accepted definitions yes, he's a serial killer, but I don't know that I can include him in the serial killer mindset of an Iceman, who seemed to really enjoy his vocation. And yet there was a day when contract killers were excluded from serial killer definitions as well, because of an assumed lack of apparent psychological gratification. These days The Iceman's lack of empathy and sadistic pleasure is more than enough to qualify, much like The Unabomber's disinterest in the bodies he might leave behind.

Both these men are clearly atypical murderers. They are both technically serial killers. Let's figure out how far out of norm they are.

COMMUNICATION FROM KILLERS

Serial killers are not all the same. Some serial killers are more than satisfied to blend into the background of their environments in order to evade detection and ply their trade unnoticed. It's certainly more efficient to not appear on a front page or a news show with a scary nickname, motivating law enforcement, politicians, and society to find you.

Long-term cold cases that have been recently discovered are examples of this. Joseph DeAngelo, Samuel Little and a plethora of other killers remained undetected for years. Many killers who were eventually found after successful careers accomplished this with a disinterest in attention.

As well, many have had no interest in fame or publicity after heading to prison. Books, interviews, and participation in documentaries don't interest them. Some feel this extra attention could threaten their safety, and rightfully so.

However, it seems the default personality of the serial murderer is one of arrogance, hubris, and a need for attention. Dennis Rader (the BTK Killer) missed the limelight so much he managed to come out of retirement loudly enough to get caught. Other convicted killers have a slate of interviews available on YouTube such as Arthur Shawcross, Joel Rifkin and even Dahmer from *Inside Edition* and Gacy on a news show. The motivation and success in getting their personal stories out in the public eye is another trait shared by Kuklinski and Kaczynski.

THE ICEMAN SPEAKS. AND SPEAKS. AND...

Richard Kuklinski did not get cheated when it came to screen time.

Kuklinski willingly participated in not one, not two, but three HBO specials that highlighted the up close and personal interviews that grew his fame and legend. *The Iceman Tapes: Conversations with a Killer* (1992), *The Iceman Confesses: Secrets of a Mafia Hitman* (2001), and *The Iceman and the Psychiatrist* (with Park Dietz) in 2003 were big hits and very popular documentaries.

Additional interviews, notably by Phillip Carlo (known for his exhaustive book on the Night Stalker), were productive as well. He spent nearly 250 hours with Kuklinski for his book *The Ice Man: Confessions of a Mafia Contract Killer* in 2006.

These pieces of access to his mind certainly allowed Kuklinski to roll in the dirt of fame. But they were not without analytic value.

It was established that Kuklinski's upbringing was horrific and damaging beyond imagination. A Carl Panzram-type figure, he was horribly bullied and abused throughout his young life. He admittedly carried a thirst for revenge, power, and retaliatory violence for anyone he could find the excuse to administer it to. He firmly decided that he would never be disrespected again. And the main person for this creation of a sociopathic homicidal machine? His father. According to Jim Goad, "nearly all Richard's hatred hinged on his father's endless beatings and ritual humiliation."

Richard Kuklinski's father, you see, routinely beat his wife in front of the children. He would also beat Richard and his brother Florian until they were out cold. In 1940 he beat Florian to death and forced his family to lie that he'd fallen downstairs, resulting in his demise.

One clip of an interview was most telling. In it, he spoke with forensic psychiatrist and serial murder expert Dr. Park Dietz, who noted it seemed that he made Kuklinski angry with a comment. The Iceman admitted this, as well as admitting that he felt some of those old triggers ("feeling flushed") that would normally motivate him to take physical retribution on the offender. He wondered aloud why he felt that way, stating, "you've got me annoyed wit' you now, that's the truth…. It's just, ah, curious to myself why… why it happened… I don't know why it happened." Finally, he concluded it was about being challenged, judged and embarrassment. About being publicly criticized and humiliated. And that was all about "of course, my father."

Another item from an interview with Phillip Carlo revealed Kuklinski's duality of personality, treating his family with extraordinary love while being capable of committing horrific murders. Carlo explained Kuklinski's history of feeding human beings to rats. Kuklinski reportedly did this seven times and filmed it. He explained that "the mark had to suffer. That was called for. But then I started wondering why this doesn't bother me. Why doesn't this trouble me? I was kind of self-analyzing myself and watched the videos and thought… why isn't this bothering me?"

Richard Kuklinski's conclusion was that he needed help.

As well, public interviews with Kuklinski's family members, including his wife Barbara and children Merrill and Christen gave insight to Kuklinski's remarkable coexistence of both love and physical control-based violence for his wife, and his loving treatment of his family.

Richard Kuklinski's exhibition of duality in his personality and psychology was extreme, even for a serial killer.

TED KACZYNSKI SPOKE AT LENGTH

The Unabomber joined Kuklinski in this atypical pair of killers who needed to be heard.

Kaczynski's downfall was essentially generated by his 35k word 1995 manifesto, *Industrial Society and Its Future*, which outlined his outrage at tech society at the cost of the wilderness. The manifesto provided the ideological foundation of his mail bomb domestic terror campaign, which was orchestrated to protect the wilderness by initiating the collapse of industrial society. Ted offered to cease his campaign of bombing and violence and murder if his screed was published, hopefully garnering the attention it deserved. While it certainly earned a lot of attention and debate among scholars and activists, his violent actions always overshadowed his philosophy.

US Attorney General Janet Reno went along with the plan, hoping someone would recognize the writing. It was printed in 1995 in supplements to the Washington Post and the New York Times. This did result in Kaczynski's brother, Donald, recognizing the writings and turned Ted in to the FBI.

Other media productions, including a 2020 Netflix docuseries *Unabomber: In His Own Words*, also offered glimpses to his personality and motivation, including pondering joining forces with Muslim terrorists, considering if there were "sufficient common ground there for any sort of alliance."

As well, a little-known interview by *Blackfoot Valley Dispatch* from 1999 added more, as it essentially stayed away from Kaczynski's terroristic violent acts and concentrated on his life as a recluse in Montana, including his deliberate removal from society and attempt to be as self-sufficient as possible. It offers bits about Ted not often discussed.

One quote, I think, was notable. When asked about whether he was self-sufficient, he said "complete self-sufficiency was a goal that I wanted to attain eventually, but with the shrinking of the wild country and the crowding-in of people around me, I got to feeling that there wasn't any point in it anymore, and my interests turned in other directions."

He went on to point out that "another thing I learned was the importance of having purposeful work to do. I mean really purposeful work – life-and-death stuff.... There is nothing more satisfying than the fulfillment and self-confidence that this kind of self-reliance brings. In connection with this, one loses most of one's fear of death."

Ted Kaczynski rejected an insanity defense but later attempted suicide in his cell in 1998. He was diagnosed with paranoid schizophrenia which led to the plea bargain that enabled him to avoid a death sentence.

Another part of Ted's psychological history includes his taking parts of a three-year experiment at Harvard. In an article by Meredith Worthen, Ted refers to this experience as a traumatic and catastrophic event in his development. He participated in a psychological experiment led by Henry Murray while at Harvard, designed to discover the limits of psychic deconstruction through weekly encounters with humiliation. The effects of this study on a boy who entered Harvard University at 16 could easily had inflicted permanent damage on him. Ted Kaczynski himself describes this as "the worst experience of his life."

Ted didn't seem to exhibit the duality that Richard did. There was no apparent double life in his history. It's telling that Kaczynski resoundingly rejected any claim of him being insane, from his brother's accusations to his in-trial defense. He has never wavered from this, much like terrorist Andres Breivik. Ted Kaczynski believes in his heart there's a logic in his actions, even if most of society would disagree.

REFERENCES

Blackfoot Valley Dispatch. (2001). An interview with Ted Kaczynski. *The Anarchist Library*. theanarchistlibrary.org.

Carlo, Phillip. (2006). *The Ice Man: Confessions of a Mafia contract killer.* New York, NY. St. Martin's Paperbacks.

CNN transcripts. (2006, June 26). CNN Larry King Live. *CNN*. transcripts.cnn.com.

Ferranti, Seth. (2017). *Cold Blooded Killer. Real Crime Magazine*, issue #21.

Kaczynski, Ted. (1995). *Industrial Society and its Future.* (essay).

Goad, Jim. (2021, March 21). Richard Kuklinski: The mafia "Iceman" and his stone-cold heart. *Thought Catalog*. thoughtcatalog.com.

Hudson Reporter. (2006, July 23). Date me or I'll kill your mother. Ex-wife of notorious 'Ice Man' talks about years with mob killer. *Hudson Reporter Archive*. hudsonreporter.com.

Inside the Criminal Mind (with John Walsh). (1992). Fox. (documentary).

Martin, Douglas. (2006, March 9). Richard Kuklinski, 70, a killer of many people and many ways, dies. *The New York Times*. www.nytimes.com.

"Operation Iceman" nabs murderer Richard Kuklinski. (2021/1986, December 17). This day in history. *History*. www.history.com.

Ray, Michael. (ND). Ted Kaczynski, American criminal. *Britannica*. britannica.com.

Reilly, Patrick. (2021, December 23). Unabomber Ted Kaczynski moved to prison medical facility from max security prison. *New York Post*. https://nypost.com.

Schager, Nick. (2020, February 22). Netflix's 'Unabomber: In his own words' reveals Ted Kaczynski's plan to team up with Muslim terrorists. *Daily Beast*. thedailybeast. com.

The Iceman and the Psychiatrist. (2003). America Undercover. Home Box Office.

The Iceman Confesses: Secrets of a Mafia hitman (2001). America Undercover. Home Box Office.

The Iceman Tapes. Conversations with a killer. (1992). America Undercover. Home Box Office.

Watts, Amanda & Jones, Kay. (2021, December 23). 'Unabomber' Ted Kaczynski transferred to a prison medical facility in North Carolina. *CNN Lite*. lite.cnn.com.

Werner, Anna. (2016, May 23). 'Unabomber' eager to tell his story from prison, with conditions. *CBS SF BayArea KPIX 5*. https://sanfrancisco.cbslocal.com.

Worthen, Meredith. (2020, October 8). What is the Unabomber's life like now? *Biography*. biography.com.

CHAPTER 6

The Dog Told me to Do It.
Who exactly are these killers?

"I remember being told as a kid, you cut off the head and the body dies. The body is nothing without the head... well, that's not quite true, there's a lot left in the girl's body without the head."

-Ed Kemper

One of the most interesting parts of teaching a Serial Murder class is finding out what people think a "serial murderer" is. Previous chapters have acknowledged the debate of whether some murderers qualify as a serial killer, including Ed Gein, Ted Kaczynski, Richard Kuklinski and even Charles Manson. I've been teaching for a couple decades now, wrote my first book on serial murder in 1996 and I think I've decided I'm pretty sure I don't know the answer.

Professor Steven Egger, my first teacher in Serial Murder, put it best once: "The more I study this subject, the more I realize how little I know."

One exercise I like to do in my class is on the first night, I have everyone give me a one or two sentence "definition of serial murder," with no rules. At the end of the semester, I have them do it again. It's very interesting to compare them 16 weeks of study later.

Not long ago, I read a description of what a serial killer might be in one of the many books I've amassed. In it, the person penning the Foreword stated, in comparison to other murderers, "the mass murderer is entirely different. He is always abnormal." He also says that this killer "thinks no more about taking a life than I do of drinking a glass of wine." He notes that the author of the book has "performed the difficult task of analyzing the methods and motives of a handful of rascals who reached infamy by sustained careers of murder."

Written by John Douglas? By Robert Ressler? Published last year? Five years ago? Ten?

That excerpt is from the book *Mass Murder*, authored by L.C. Douthwaite. Foreword by George Dilnot.

In 1929.

I think like Dilnot, describing the serial murderer is better than trying to define him. Or her.

Particularly in an era where they hadn't even thought of the term "serial killer" yet.

I like to explain to people that I believe serial murder is a mindset, a consistent psychological motivation that can be identified to the point of categorizing it in the American Psychiatric Association's *Diagnostic and Statistical Manual of Mental Disorders* (DSM). I've been a big believer in that litmus-test consideration of numbers of successful kills to be erroneous although it's almost always the first thing people list when defining the serial killer. My position has always been that a serial killer is determined by his intent, not his success rate.

But who is he? Or her? How many do they kill? What do they look like? How wrong are most people about… everything?

SO HOW ABOUT THOSE NUMBERS?

For quite some time, a common belief was that the definition of a serial killer was someone who had committed at least three murders at separate times, differentiating them from mass murderers. According to the FBI, Title 18 of the U.S. Code in 1998 defined "serial killings" as a "series of three or more killings… having common characteristics such as to suggest the reasonable possibility that the crimes were committed by the same actor or actors." It was also considered that serial murder "required a temporal separation between the different murders, which was described as: separate occasions, cooling-off period, and emotional cooling off period." Later, at an FBI multi-disciplinary Symposium in San Antonio, Texas, a definition was crafted in order to be utilized by law enforcement, which I'll discuss upcoming.

Prolific expert author and criminal psychology professor Eric Hickey has always preferred a broad definition of serial murder, stating in 2016 the definition is "to include all types of serial killers, the definition of serial murder must clearly be as broad as possible."

Dr. Steven Egger on the other hand, always favored a more narrow, specific overall definition of the serial killer. Included in that was an initial definition he suggested in 1983 when he stated that "serial murder occurs when one or more individuals... commit a second murder and/or subsequent murder." (1990) He went on to re-state this number threshold within an expanded, 7-point refined definition in 2002 and beyond. He details factors including relationship between killer and victim, motives, locations, and victim characteristics.

From the beginning I thought the concept of three minimum kills was deeply flawed. Westley Allen Dodd wasn't a serial killer in the 80s because the kid he scooped up at *Honey I Shrunk the Kids* made too much noise and he wasn't able to get him home to rape and hang in his closet? To push him over that magical #3 mark? Ed Gein wasn't a serial killer because he only killed 2? Did he need to move to a bigger town? His number totals were more of a reflection of his mental abilities and opportunity than his desire and motivation. He wasn't a serial killer in 2001 but suddenly was in 2007? The arbitrary nature of this determination always seemed counter-productive in its use.

But Andrei Chikatilo was, because he'd killed so many in a culture in Russia that made apprehending such a monster incredibly difficult? I don't think so.

Serial killers are often captured by tremendous Police work. Sometimes, they are caught by blind luck. A broken tail light. Running a red light. Sloppy disposal. A self-destructive need for attention. These events often stop a killer's career in its tracks, one that could have been another Bundy, another Green River Killer. But they are external influences that dramatically affect a killer's final kill total, which often have nothing to do with their need or intention to kill.

The single reason that there are so few child serial killers is that they aren't very good at anything just yet. Actual youthful serial killers like Jesse Pomeroy or Mary Bell are the exception, to have been able to successfully "kill 2 or more in separate events." Kids are inherently sloppy, fail to plan and get caught quickly. It doesn't mean that an Eric Smith wouldn't have killed several if he improved his success rate instead of admitting to his brutal murder of Derrick Robie days after the crime.

In a 2014 journal of *Aggression and Violent Behavior*, Adjorlolo and Chan published an article, "*The Controversy of Defining Serial Murder: Revisited.*" Within, the authors examined the various elements used to define the serial killer. Among these elements was what I'd consider the most elementary: minimum number of kills. The authors conclude with a minimum number of 2, reflecting the FBI definition, and prescribe a motive of personal motivation. However, the review takes into account a wide range of motivations and minimum numbers, many of which are 3 or more.

Some suggest the motivation behind "the move to expand the pool of serial murder cases" was started in terms of politics and resources. The suggestion was made that the FBI backed a lower threshold due to resources and funding priorities. Simply put, the idea followed that if there were "thousands" rather than "hundreds" of serial killer victims in the US, expanded resources from Congress could be demanded. As well, if serial murder was redefined to be repetitive murders after 2 kills, "the problem – and thus the need for additional funding – would only seem to be magnified," stated Fox and Levin in their text *Extreme Killing*.

In August/September 2005, the FBI's Behavioral Analysis Unit-2 (BAU-2) held a symposium in San Antonio, Texas, inviting serial killer experts to determine a more comprehensive serial murder definition. Many factors were considered and reported upon. One result was a working definition, stating, *Serial Murder: The unlawful killing of two or more victims by the same offender(s), in separate events.* It should be noted that within the BAU-2's report, they mentioned a factor for lower numbers in a working definition: "… since the definition was to be utilized by law enforcement, a lower number of victims would allow law enforcement more flexibility in committing resources to a potential serial murder investigation."

However, the ability to create subcategories within serial killers based on numbers, is always an option for the researchers, just as breaking out spree killers from the overall definition is done by many today.

Fox and Levin define the serial killer as one who kills a minimum of 4 victims separated by a cooling-off period of at least 24 hours. They say that a benefit of opting for this high victim threshold is that it is consistent with the definition of mass murder.

Fox, Levin & Fridel opined that

> It is difficult to say for certain why such a broad approach was favored by the
> FBI's behavioral analysts; it may simply be a matter of resources and

funding priorities. Broadening the scope of the problem, even artificially, may help law enforcement secure additional resources for investigating homicides (2019)

The authors feel "scholars have been all too willing to play along with this newer criterion, even though it casts doubt on much of the research that has been accomplished to date."

There are a couple of issues regarding numbers in play here:

1. The minimum number of kills required to qualify as a serial killer in a specific researcher's serial murderer definition and

2. The entire body count by an offender who may or may not be considered a "serial killer" by one researcher could be included or removed from another database or study based on factors usually involving motivation like gang activity or behaviors or concepts such as a "cooling off period."

The idea that some researchers include more offenders, such as with Hickey's broad definition that denotes a serial killer as an offender "who kills over time" based on budgetary benefits, suggests, critically, that money is more significant than the purity of a definition.

This is an interesting suggestion, but as someone whose never had any funding, I can't say with certainty how I feel about it. I believe recent researchers' propensity to include more offenders in the pool of "serial killers" by ignoring motivation or eliminating concepts like "cooling off periods" and "spree kills" are unfortunate, but I must believe they are a result of esoteric perspective and personal bias rather than a financial end game. And as someone who strongly believes that a serial killer personality can exist after the murder of just one victim, I look at my own global outlook and I would argue my overall population of offenders and victims would be significantly smaller, not bigger, even when including killers of one rather than 3, provided you include motive along with numbers for inclusion. My general parameters for inclusion into the serial killer club are much narrower and always have been, suppressing numbers as a result.

DEBATING NUMBERS REQUIRED TO BE A SERIAL KILLER

One thing about serial murder... there's plenty to argue about, and plenty of people willing to take that argument on. A couple of friends, colleagues, and authors I know, Enzo Yaksic and Steve Daniels, and I've enjoyed discussing this whole "minimum" number of victims, or "successful kills" required be the officially considered a serial killer. Daniels explains:

> A number of years ago, at a conference in Boston, Steve and I met with Enzo Yaksic, founder of the Serial Homicide Expertise and Information Sharing Collaborative, and the Atypical Homicide Research Group. I have found discussions with Enzo and Steve to be of great value in my previous career as a high-risk parole agent and my current as Chair, Cold Case Review Team, Wisconsin Association of Homicide Investigators.
>
> Obviously, the conversation/debate focused on serial murder. One interesting area focused on was gauging serial murder qualitatively not quantitively. How many victims does a killer need to have to be a serial killer? Originally, the FBI offered three, then reduced the number to two, but the discussion then focused on possibly one victim, particularly if the murder showed certain select signs of a sexual homicide. Giannangelo, in his book: *REAL LIFE MONSTERS*, took the discussion even further suggesting a "homicidal pattern disorder," offering a killer could show signs of this disorder with one "kill". Also, proffered was what if a killer's career was interrupted after one murder by arrest, prison, mental health commitment or death? This interrupted offender was on a path toward multiple killings. The night was spent engaging in discussing: types of serial killers, what makes a homicide sexual, what indicators are evident in a homicide? Enzo was so enthralled with the discussion he went on to write a juried/published journal article on our discussions of how many victims are required to be a serial killer.

The argument generally starts at 2 and ends at 3, based on history. However, we have felt that the serial killer is a personality, a motivation, that cannot begin at the third kill. In fact, we have dared to suggested that an offender can be a serial killer with only one successful kill. Is this an esoteric concept? Perhaps, but it's another great excuse to spend another night debating about serial killers.

Those that believe it should be 3 or 4 successful kills or more would cry foul at this notion. Researchers Emma E. Fridel and James Alan Fox stressed this point in their Psychology of Violence journal article *Too Few Victims: Finding the Optimal Minimum Victim Threshold for Defining Serial Murder*. There they debate the FBI's decision to land on 2 as a minimum kill count and conclude that "Two-victim offenders differ significantly from all other serial killers in terms of motive, partnership, and crime scene behaviors, and arguably should not be pooled into a single population."

Fridel & Fox's displeasure of the FBI settling on a 2-victim threshold over the previous three or four victims minimum established by "most scholars," resulted in their statement that there still was "no consensus" on the definition, and that they "suggest what appears to be the optimal threshold based on distinguishing attributes." They concluded that

> A minimum victim threshold of at least three should be used, separating potential or would-be serial killers from those who are characterized by more extreme levels of violent behavior.

I think it's fair to conclude that the greater the kills (or more, according to Fridel and Fox) can often be subdivided into a group capable of more extreme violent behavior. This is setting aside the luck factor, such as Chikatilo v. Dodd. Or maybe it's more than luck; it's more a factor such as resiliency, identified by Yaksic's group's research.

Another interesting article by Yaksic entitled *The Folly of Counting Bodies* in a 2018 journal *Aggression and Violent Behavior* debates the Friedel/Fox article and concludes that their method discounts thousands of serial homicide offenders due to the absence of information on formative events and disregard intent and markers associated with serial homicide. He further states the result would "curtail the foray of new researchers into an area rife with potential discoveries while also restricting efforts by law enforcement organizations to form task forces to intervene earlier in an offender's career."

Yaksic notes that the

> …undue emphasis placed on body count, a niche aspect of serial homicide research, by the authors in *Too Few Victims* has the capacity to further alienate disparate groups of researchers and practitioners from each other and from those law enforcement officers they are aiming to help.

Yaksic, et al. (2021) also describe an interesting consideration of the concept of aspiring, probable and successful serial murderers within the concept of including offenders as "serial killers." They "hypothesize that probable serial killers will be older offenders with pleasure-based motives that have a complete understanding of what they are and act logically and grounded in reality after minimal ideation." They also note that aspiring and probable (denoted as killers of 2) have more traits in common with the successful (3 or more kills) serial killers than the "one-off" murderers.

In contrast, Fox and Levin in their text, refer to the Friedel/Fox study, offer their own subtypes: potential or wannabe serial killers (those with only 2 victims), typical serial killers with 3 to 7 victims and prolific serial killers, with at least 8 successful kills.

These studies also suggest:

- The population size and general traits of serial killers change substantially depending on the choice of minimum victim threshold.

- Including two-victim offenders nearly doubles or triples the total number of serial killers in comparison to three- and four-victim cutoffs.

- While including these offenders produces populations similar in age and race, the two-victim minimum reduces the proportion of perpetrators that engage in stereotypical serial killer behaviors, particularly killing with a partner, raping, torturing, taking totems, and killing for enjoyment.

Clearly this argument goes much deeper than journal articles and personal intuition, but it's one that will always be fun to continue. And knowing the participants, as well as new blood involved with each argument, it will always be interesting.

BEYOND JUST NUMBERS: MOTIVATION

It's stated in the BAU-2's report that "Motivation was another central element discussed in various definitions; however, attendees felt motivation did not belong in a general definition, as it would make the definition overly complex." This is understandable, as I suppose it would constrict a general database of multiple murderers which could be categorized from a raw grouping.

However, I still cannot get past the consideration of motivation and my idea of the serial killer personality. Brooks, et al's 1988 definition (as quoted by Egger) referenced "quite often the motive is psychological" and "sadistic, sexual overtones." The definition at least "quite often" left room for other considerations.

There was a time that many of us eliminated material gain as a qualifier for the serial killer. Dr. Egger in 2002 echoed a common refrain when he stated, "the motive is not for material gain; it is for the murderer's desire to have power and dominance over the victims." I included this specific point about material gain in both of my books in 1996 and 2012.

In both books, I suggested a formal diagnostic listing for the *DSM*, titled Homicidal Pattern Disorder. This included the point that serial murder was "not motivated by monetary gain." It made sense at the time, and it was the current belief. I'd have to drop that one today.

There was a time when I would argue the murders of H.H. Holmes, many of which were related to stealing money or property weren't about monetary gain, and that they were about asserting his power and control. Today I must acknowledge motivations for financial windfall to simply be part of his motivation to kill some people… some people who might not have been in his crosshairs otherwise. Egger, like most of us, separated motivation of material gain from those of power and dominance. I now must accept that it's very difficult to separate these motivations from one another. These killers are routinely included in serial killer databases that work from the FBI's definition of 2 kills at different times, without regard to motivation, so it's important to be consistent. It's simply true that a serial killer can have multiple motivations, and financial gain, seen in Holmes, Aileen Wuornos and even the D.C. Snipers (setting aside the spree killer argument) are clear factors along with others. And killing for financial gain with premeditation, like Holmes, or by chance or necessity like some spree killers such as Starkweather/Fugate or Cunanan, are still kills that occur in a series and should be included.

Another thought was the application of my description to the female serial murderer. For many years it made sense to think that "female killers are just different," but as time goes by, the more I believe the female serial killer is less and less different from the male counterpart. Different killers may have different particular traits, but a definition should try to identify everything that is consistent and save discussing the detail differences for later. The fact is, historically, many female serial killers were guilty of killing for money and that never fit the traditional narrative. Eliminating the financial aspect of the narrative makes female killers far less different than the prototypical male killer in the end.

Females also bust the myth that serial killers kill primarily strangers. Again, that's most often the case, but when you look at the number of Black Widows out there, it's hard to call a string of husbands "strangers." Or other family members. It's also not uncommon for serial murderers to have had personal relationships with some members on their victim list, such as Herbert Mullin and Donald Harvey.

Overemphasized factors such as sex and sadism simply don't always apply. Eliminating revenge or hatred or concealing other crimes don't make any sense anymore, either. Just considering some serial rapists who might have been caught and even served time because of the testimony of a surviving victim, it would not make sense to eliminate an offender as a serial killer just because he chooses to eliminate the possibility of a woman who could testify against him. This is not killing for power, or sadism, or sexual pleasure. It's expediency. It's being pragmatic. It's a staggering indifference to life and a stunning example of the complete lack of empathy a psychopath or a sociopathic killer can display, but it's certainly serial killing.

As a serial killer I interviewed in person told me once: "It's like stealing a car. When you are done, you get rid of the car. Right?"

Incidentally, that killer was once arrested and convicted based on the testimony of a surviving sexual assault victim. That wasn't going to happen again.

So, while I really want to include some modicum of motive in my serial killer definition, one that reflects power or control, or obvious psychological disorder or sadism or a deep-seated need to kill, I don't think I can make the case that it will always apply to all serial killers. Unclear motivation killers like Texas serial bomber Mark Conditt, eliminate any such broad global assumptions.

I think that may be the most significant fact I've learned over the years, and the one most driven home by my interviews done for my last book. You cannot apply every trait or every factor in every case. They are individual cases with individual sets of circumstances, personalities, motivations, and pathologies. You need to identify them, specifically.

REVISITING A DEFINITION AND HOMICIDAL PATTERN DISORDER

While the FBI's symposium did appear to set a standard for laws enforcement's use of a definition of serial murder, I think it's fair, in my third book, to take another swing at it. (Baseball jokes about 3 strikes not required) As this topic evolves, I believe we all continue to re-define our positions.

I feel I must change my overall format. Given the way experts in the field have added more killers based on numbers and no concern for motivation, I'll allow for that doctrine. I do think the FBI's definition is a decent starting point, but I want to add the caveat that there are distinct subtypes of serial murderers that should viewed specifically in their own right. I still clarify that the serial murderer personality is based on intent for repeat murder, not of success rate.

Therefore, my 2022 definition of Serial Murder looks like this:

Serial Murder:

The unlawful intentional killing of at least one individual coupled with a successful or legitimate unsuccessful attempt at intentionally killing additional victims, in separate events. They can be committed alone or in tandem with others. Motives and psychological makeup are determined for specific subsets.

Subsets could include but are not restricted to:
Spree killers, killers with mental illness of any level, sexually motivated killers, uncommon motivation killers, organization-related killers, and unspecified.

Victims will often be grouped by a commonality, but it is possible a commonality could be the randomness and apparent disorganization of the victim pool.

I still believe in the concept of diathesis-stress in the creation of many serial killers, which is the combination of biological predisposition and psychological trauma. I also still believe in my long-held theory that there is in fact a consistent psychological mindset of a serial killer type, which I've described as Homicidal Pattern Disorder and suggested for inclusion in the *DSM-3, 4* and *5* over the years. However, from years of study and from feedback from actual serial murderers, I don't know that I can include every serial killer case in these theories because of the removal of motivation from qualifiers. I can only say that diathesis-stress is one route to a journey that ends with a serial murderer, but we cannot say all. I can also say that the existence of Homicidal Pattern Disorder does in fact describe a certain type of serial murderer's psychology, one that is identifiable and consistent for research purposes.

The classification also fits in the *International Classification of Diseases* (ICD) category of Other habit and impulse disorders. This describes the person as "repeatedly failing to resist impulses to carry out the behaviour. There is a prodromal period of tension with a feeling of release at the time of the act."

I continue to see the obsessive, ritualistic cycle as analogous to the alcoholism Bundy compared it to, and therefore it seems like a behavioral addiction. This leaves elements B and C unchanged. I did remove some specific disqualified motivations as discussed previously.

My DSM diagnostic criteria for Homicidal Pattern Disorder, listed under Disruptive, Impulse Control and Conduct Disorders, for 2022 would be:

313.99 (F63.8) Homicidal Pattern Disorder:

A. Unlawful, intentional successful killing of at least one person coupled with a successful or legitimate unsuccessful attempt at killing one or more additional victims, in separate occasions.

B. Tension or affective arousal at some time before the act.

C. Pleasure, gratification, or relief in successful completion of the act, either immediately or in reflection.

D. Understanding of the illegality of actions and effort to avoid apprehension.

Comorbidity with personality disorders such as Antisocial (see *DSM-5*), Obsessive-Compulsive, Narcissistic, or other disorders such as Intermittent Explosive or Reactive Attachment Disorder is expected.

Antisocial Personality Disorder within the *DSM-5* alternative model specified with psychopathic features is most applicable to Homicidal Pattern Disorder:

> A distinct variant often termed psychopathy is marked by a lack of anxiety or fear and by a bold interpersonal style that may mask maladaptive behaviors. This psychopathic variant is characterized by low levels of anxiousness (Negative affectivity) and withdrawal (Detachment) and high levels of attention seeking. (Antagonism) High attention seeking and low withdrawal capture the social potency, (assertive/dominant) component of psychopathy,

whereas low anxiousness captures the stress immunity (emotional stability/resilience) component.

RACE AND SERIAL MURDER

In Chapter 8 I specifically look at the latest in female killers, so I'll leave gender for later. However, while we are talking about numbers, in June 2019, 79-year-old Samuel Little, in failing health and serving three consecutive life sentences in California, started increasing his lifetime count by confessing to dozens more. His count increased to more than 60 kills, eclipsing what was previously considered the highest number of serial kills in the U.S. in terms of guilty pleas: Gary Ridgeway with 49. Given the moving target that total number of kills assigned to many, many serial killers—Bundy's numbers are routinely dismissed as underestimated, and even Gacy's count continues to rise as recently as 2021—debates about the standings on the current Serial Murder Leaderboard will continue.

However, Samuel, before his death, brought up another topic: the Black serial murderer. But… serial killers are White males… right?

We all remember Sigourney Weaver's character in the 1995 film *Copycat*, a professor making all the White males under 30 in a lecture hall stand up… and pointing out that "this is what 90% of serial killers look like." How many movies, documentaries and articles echoed this belief? And, while I've heard this opening scene to the film referenced in the occasional article commenting on serial murder in America, never ever have I read how utterly wrong her generalizations were and how universally accepted they continued to be.

Trends in serial murder statistics show clearly that serial murder is down significantly since the Golden Age of Serial Murder of the 70s and 80s. Those trends also show a marked increase in the percentage of serial killers that are Black over time as well.

Is there an increase in Black killers, or in detecting them?

NUMBERS

Let's look at actual numbers regarding race and serial killers, beyond the myths.

Samuel Little. (2014, Los Angeles, USA. Damian Dovarganes/AP/Shutterstock.)

In recent research, complied by Radford University's Dr. Mike Aamodt in his serial killer database, numbers show a U.S. Black/White statistical history break down as follows: (serial murderers active within decades)

1970s: 60.7 % White; 33.6 % Black

1980s: 52.6 % White; 37.7 % Black

1990s: 41.0 % White; 47.0 % Black

2000s: 31.0 % White; 54.3 % Black

2010s: 31.3 % White; 57.2 % Black

(Source: Radford/FGCU Serial Killer Database, updated 6/26/2020)

Please note that all stats tend to evolve, but these numbers show minimal changes since 2015. Also, keep in mind many of the available statistics include slight differences in populations (U.S. only, 2 or 3 victim minimums, gender, year inclusions, etc.) so numbers have small variance when approximated and compared.

Statistics provided by Enzo Yaksic in 2022, founder of the Atypical Homicide Research Group (AHRG), revealed the following:

Between 2011 and 2021, there have been 381 U.S.-based serial murderers (104 two-victim killings, 115 three or more victim killings, 115 sprees, 20 female murderers, and 27 teams). This is a decrease from the 823 serial murderers who operated in the US in the 1980s, which was the peak period for serial murders in the US.

Almost 50% of serial murderers are Black, and 41% are White.

I should note my repeated citations of Enzo's research in both the discussions on numbers and race in this chapter. This is because his work is groundbreaking and exhaustive and neither conversation is complete without his contributions. (*See his essay later in this chapter*)

Spree killers are often conflated with serial killers by researchers these days; others still look at them as a specific category. Researchers Katherine Ramsland and Mark Safarik released an excellent book on spree killers in 2020 which hopefully moves towards clarifying this classification for criminologists and law enforcement researchers. Some researchers feel the differentiation between spree and serial to be less useful when considering the many killers who kill over shorter periods of time. Maybe it's semantics, but spree killers in my mind are a very specific type of serial killer. I still think it's fair to look at the spree killer psychology separately, which often evidences a "beginning" and an "end" due to a psychic disturbance or event, unlike longer term serial killers who often offend over the course of years. Their patience and deliberate, meticulous planning are unlike any spree killer, whose apparent mental disturbance causes his behavior to be more spontaneous, disorganized, and emotional, which is a different target to apprehend.

BLACK SERIAL MURDERERS IN MEDIA & RESEARCH

In 1993, Philip Jenkins published an article in the *American Journal of Criminal Justice*, *African-Americans and Serial Homicide*. This topic, was, in a word, underexamined in the day.

Jenkins' article abstract stated:

> African Americans are usually over-represented among offenders arrested in "normal" homicide cases, making up a considerably larger proportion than would be expected from the Black presence in the population at large. Among serial murderers, however, African Americans are much less in evidence— perhaps one-fifth or less of known American serial killers are Black. It may be that African Americans are in fact less involved in serial murder activity than are Anglo Whites or Hispanics; but it must also be asked whether this is simply an impression gained from the ways in which serial murder activity is identified and investigated. For several reasons, law enforcement agencies might be less likely to seek or find evidence of serial murder activity where the victims are Black. As homicide is primarily an intra-racial crime, this would then mean that Black serial killers would be far more likely to escape detection.

So, Jenkins felt Black serial killers historically were more often undetected (and therefore less counted) due to the "less-dead" (per Steven Egger definition) status of the victims, who were more likely to be Black. It's an interesting observation, although White serial killers that preferred Black victims such as Jeffrey Dahmer and Larry Bright prove an exception.

In 2006, Yaksic challenged previous research and assumptions suggesting Black males only represented 20% of serial killers in a presentation that found that 46% of American serial killers since 1995 have been Black, a similar amount as were White.

Author Allan Branson published another article on Black serial killers, *African American Serial Killers: Over-Represented Yet Underacknowledged* in the *Howard Journal of Crime and Statistics* in 2013. He stated there have been 90 Black serial killers on record from 1945 to that date, yet their "notoriety and celebrity are absent from America's popular cultural landscape." He stated the "unquestioned ethnocentric profile of the serial killer is a White male was created by the FBI and subsequent media portrayals have reinforced this myth."

Author Molly Wolfe asked some hard questions in a 2020 shoutoutuk.org article *Serial Killers are fascinating – except when they're Black*. She rightly noticed that Black serial killers simply don't seem included in today's "collective obsession with serial killer documentaries and films."

She notes a recent documentary film that humanized and gushed over Ted Bundy's positive attributes while ignoring his monstrous acts and character. This complaint is not a new one, as the fawning new aficionados that sprouted over Zac Efron's dreamy film portrayal of the apparently irresistible Ted (also referenced by Wolfe) seemed to inflame the annoyance of many people disgusted with what appeared to be a sympathetic and heroic depiction of a vile predator. But those complaints were about hero worshipping killers; Wolfe's point was that it was the depiction of the smart, handsome White man, a role not found with a Black protagonist.

Wolfe also references *My Friend Dahmer*, a film based on a graphic comic novel on Jeffrey Dahmer's story. Again, the complaint is about the glorification of a murderer, "stating if you do something brilliantly awful, maybe they will make a film about you."

While I agree with all of this, it makes the valid point that high profile criminals and murderers have always been the subjects of film, TV, and magazine covers. The White serial killers that have long been the favorites of film (Bundy-Gacy) are generally those from the Golden Age of Serial Murder in the 70s and 80s, when there were more White serial killers active. But now that the racial numbers have balanced out, maybe what we see on the screen will in fact change.

When I consider the unfairness of these stories which don't appear to have Black subjects, I must ask which stories of Black serial killers are being left out? The examples of

Ted Bundy and Jeffrey Dahmer are true, but both are compelling stories. Is it wrong that there hasn't been a feature film made of Wayne B. Williams and the child murders in Atlanta? Should there be a new film on Samuel Little, the recently crowned statistical king of the kills by the FBI? It's probably a valid question. It could also be answered by the time this question finds its way into print.

Ms. Wolfe makes strong statements, that Black serial killers are not on the screen because "White is considered goodness and when they aren't, we need to know why." She brings up if Black killers are not interesting enough and are not allowed to take center stage and the growing percentage of Black serial killers should be reflected in films and documentaries. I bring these points up because they are not far from the points made by Jenkins as far back as 1993 and Branson more recently when they felt Blacks were not thought of as being a cunning, manipulative serial killer. It's an interesting juxtaposition, as it brings out factors that must be considered uncomfortable. Wolfe says "by making films about White killers, we're celebrating them. By neglecting to acknowledge Black serial killers, they're not even a last-minute invite to the party."

While I do not doubt many of the assumptions made regarding the dearth of Black serial killers in media are true, another consideration must be considered. Let's face it, for a long time the general assumption was that serial killers were White, period and that the idea of a Black serial killer was an anomaly. This underestimation isn't confined to race; popular thought completely underestimated and ignored female serial killers as well.

One observation: The 2020 Radford Database summary of serial killer statistics does state a difference statistically in serial killer motives by race. "Enjoyment was more often a motive for Whites than African Americans whereas Gang or Criminal Enterprise activity was more often a motive for African Americans than Whites." Could media biases trend more towards serial murder cases committed for the purpose of "enjoyment" over those by "criminal enterprise," for sake of storyline as opposed to race?

It's been noted that Black serial killers don't earn the catchy nicknames that White serial killers do. Not entirely true of course. "The Grim Sleeper," AKA Lonnie Franklin, had a memorable moniker. Franklin killed at least 10 in California from 1984 to 2007 and was also convicted of rape and sexual violence. He died in 2020.

Even better, and even less known was "The Doodler," also known as the Black Doodler. Another California killer (San Francisco), he is a yet-unidentified killer who reportedly is credited for 16 kills in 1974 and '75. Trolling for victims at gay nightclubs, he earned his name after he reportedly sketched his victims' likenesses before their sexual contact and eventual murders by stabbing them.

1975 Forensic Sketch   2018 Forensic Sketch

Doodler Police sketch. (2019, San Francisco, USA. Uncredited/AP/Shutterstock.)

There's a couple issues at play here: Were (are) Black serial killers spectacularly underrepresented in the media, likely to erroneous stereotyping and potential biases? Clearly true. Were Blacks undercounted and underdetected in historical statistical summaries of serial murder, particularly before 1995? Looks like it. Reasons vary wildly. The question that seems unanswered when looking at the numbers in context is this: were prior numbers regarding Black serial killers understated due to detection error to the point where the greater numbers today do not reflect a real increase in Black serial killer percentages?

Still, researchers are aware of the demographics now, and most people you talk to on the street continue to think serial killers are usually White males.

Unless you are paying attention of course. In recent years, along with the name Samuel Little, serial killers like Gerald Brevard (Washington, DC), Perez Deshay Reed (MO, KS), Rosemary Ddlovu (South Africa), Kevin Gavin (Brooklyn, NY), Mark Goudeau (Phoenix, AZ), Masten Wanjala (Kenya), Mathew Macon (Lansing, MI), Khali

Wheeler-Weaver (New Jersey), Darren Vann (Indiana), Howell Donaldson (Seminole Heights, FL), Themba Prince Dube (Limpopo), Wellington Kachidza (Pretoria), Michael Madison (Cleveland, OH), Billy Chemirmir (Dallas, TX) and Frederick Demond Scott (Kansas City, MO) are just a taste of the Black serial killers whose crimes or trials or sentencing were in the news, briefly, yet few recognize them.

And if you look hard enough, you can find that elusive grand nickname. In January 2022, Police were investigating a minimum of 5 murders, and expecting more, of "The Shopping Cart Killer," Anthony Robinson, 35, from Virginia. "He's killed four already, and we suspect that he has more victims. He's a predator, as all serial killers are," Fairfax County Police Chief Kevin Davis said during a news conference, adding that the so-called Shopping Cart Killer does "unspeakable things with his victims." Not long after this statement, Fairfax County Police were tipped that a fifth victim from Washington DC was likely related. Other victims were positively identified at the time of that update.

Chief Davis said, "we believe there are survivors out there," as they continue to work this quickly-evolving case.

The following is an essay graciously provided by Enzo Yaksic, the brilliant researcher I've quoted so often. He is the Director of the AHRG, which maintains the Consolidated Serial Homicide Offender Database, the largest open repository for information on atypical homicide offenders.

The Profile of the Modern U.S.-Based Serial Murderer
By Enzo Yaksic

The majority of serial murder research has been conducted on the U.S. offender population due to early pioneering efforts by agents of the FBI to understand the uptick in these types of crimes during what has become known as the 'Golden Age' of serial murder. Soon after, U.S.-based scholars took an interest in the phenomenon of serial murder but were dismayed by the unavailability of a diverse cohort of subjects and a reliance on information that was not systematically collected. The involvement of a variety of parties at such a foundational moment led to siloed thinking and gave rise to a contentious atmosphere which contributed to a wide variance in early findings (Yaksic, 2015). Thus, the next section will discuss the profile of the modern serial murderer in the U.S.

The aforementioned issues bolstered the need for widely accessible and reliable data. To that end, the largest open-source serial murder database was created (Aamodt, Fox, Hickey, Hinch, Labuschagne, et al 2021) in an effort to support today's researchers. Using this data, many have since adopted the view that the modern profile of the serial murderer opposes much of the accepted tenets amassed over the years. For example, only 18% of modern-day offenders match the 'white loner' profile from the Golden Age. Modern U.S.-based serial murderers tend to be local undereducated men of average intelligence who engage in intimate partner violence, are lucky to escape apprehension, and are propelled forward by a deep sense of entitlement, fragile masculinity, easy access to firearms, and a nonchalant attitude toward using murder to attain their goals (Yaksic, 2022). This profile is contrary to the image of the uber-intelligent, traveling serial murderer who kills dozens of victims and avoids detection due to superior abilities. As human beings, serial murderers create rationalizations that aid them in killing, which is their way of subversively rejecting social norms and violating the social contract. Serial murderers often know they are psychologically and emotionally damaged, but use biological ailments as excuses, see themselves as victims of society and circumstances, and struggle with their alternate identities due to their inability to experience life normally because of personality or psychological problems (Shanafelt & Pino, 2013).

The most prevalent profile of the serial murderer in the US is a Black male with a criminal record who kills two or more victims locally with a firearm, out of anger, in the Midwest, over a 2 to 5 year period beginning and ending in young adulthood (Yaksic, 2022).

Serial murder has been a source of fascination since it was first recognized as a concept. The Golden Age of serial murder in the U.S. spanned from the peak of the phenomenon in the 1970s to the year 2000 when the prevalence of offenders began to decline. Serial murder has traditionally been perceived as strictly an American phenomenon given the higher prevalence of this crime in the U.S. Although serial murder has been studied through a U.S.-based perspective, recent years have seen new research from a global view, most notably from Germany, South Africa, Australia, Sweden, France, Italy, and India. These studies found that there are more similarities between serial murderers globally than there are racial, cultural, or ethnic differences. While most serial murderer's crimes are likely to serve selfish needs and be a large detriment to society, the average victim count across countries are small. Young female strangers were a common victim to most serial murderers, with offences committed when offenders are in their late 20s or early 30s. The majority of serial murderers significantly vary their killing methods and motives, have a criminal history, have a low economic status, or are blue-collar workers, and many have a personality or substance abuse disorder. Golden Age serial murderers in the U.S. were motivated primarily by a need for sexual gratification, but recent research has demonstrated that modern-day serial murderers are more frequently motivated by a desire to appease their anger. Around the globe, from country to country, serial murderers are ineffectual people who measure success not by the milestones common to normal people but by the metric of how sated they are by the havoc they introduce into communities.

ADDITIONAL INFLUENCE OF MEDIA ON THE TOPIC OF SERIAL MURDER

And since we brought up the subject of media…

The explosion of serial murder content in the media has never been more intense. A peek of a couple random days' offerings on your favorite streaming service could flood your palate: *Extremely Wicked, Shockingly Evil and Vile. You. The Fall. Creep. Murder Mountain. My Friend Dahmer. The Killing. Velvet Buzzsaw. Mrs. Serial Killer. The Mind of Aaron Hernandez. Mindhunter. The Valhalla Murders. Interview with a Serial Killer. Wild Wild Country. Zodiac. The Confession Killer. Inside the Criminal Mind. Conversations With a Killer: The Ted Bundy Tapes. Hush. Forensic Files. The Assassination of Gianni Versace. Nurses Who Kill. La Mante. Serial Killer with Piers Morgan. Tales of the Grim Sleeper. Bayou Blue. Cropsey. Ted Bundy: Falling for a Killer. The Jeffrey Dahmer Files. H. H. Holmes. America's First Serial Killer. Aileen: Life and Death of a Serial Killer. Killer Ratings. I survived B.T.K.: BTK and the Otero Family Murders. The Jinx: The Life and Deaths of Robert Durst. The Real 'Des': The Dennis Nilsen Story. This is the Zodiac Speaking. The Pig Farm. Night Stalker: Hunt for a Serial Killer. The Ripper. Memories of a Murderer: The Nilsen Tapes.* These are a fraction of what's out there any given day.

And mainstream networks like Investigation Discovery, History Channel, Reelz, and A&E churn out new documentaries like butter, "new" spins often on the Golden Age of Serial Murder, new first-person victim and family accounts, not to mention the insufferable new, shocking, sometimes ridiculous theories of twists and conspiracies on many of the stories you have heard for years. The raging popularity and saturation of the genre cannot be debated.

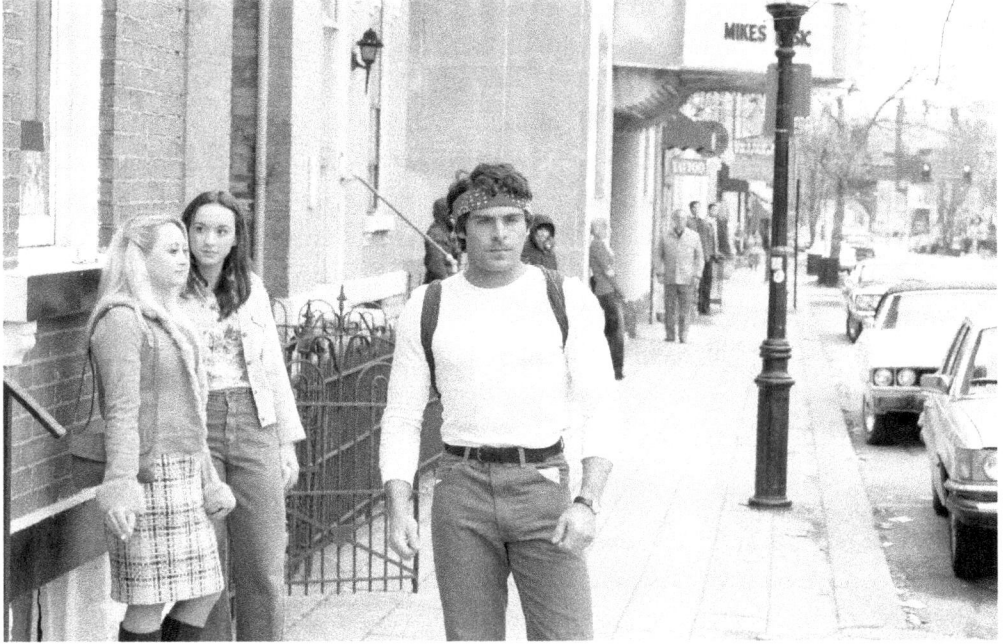

Zac Efron as Ted Bundy in the film "Extremely Wicked, Shockingly Evil and Vile."
(2019 Brian Douglas/COTA/Netflix/Kobal/Shutterstock.)

For the record, as I write this, I have A&E Network on in the background and have heard references or ads for *Invisible Monsters: Serial Killers in America, I Survived a Serial Killer, BTK: Confession of a Serial Killer* and *First Blood*, all serial killer content.

I've always been interested in the perception difference between the media portrayal of the serial murderer and the public's disconnect with reality. I've discussed the myths and misconceptions regarding race and serial killers in assumption and reality. Another idea is the concept that society "gets what they deserve" (to quote *The Joker* among others) in their behaviors and biases, in creating the serial killer. What exactly is the general public's responsibility in the creation of the serial killer?

Offenders like Carl Panzram would argue the serial killer is entirely created by the public and their mistreatment of others. Some believe society's beliefs and views about homosexuals in the 70s helped create an environment where a John Wayne Gacy could evolve and thrive.

Others would point to the objectification and abuse of women as well as the marginalization of some segments of society, which creates a veritable endless victim pool for those with a mind to murder to troll without detection. The Green River Killer might agree. Maybe Arthur Shawcross and Joel Rifkin, too.

It seems that the general public still thinks of Hannibal Lecter or some other generic White, male, evil genius from *Criminal Minds* when they picture a serial killer. I assume if *Copycat* was re-aired on your favorite streaming service, most of the people watching would listen to Sigourney Weaver's description of what a serial killer looks like and nod their heads like it's 1995.

Then I'd think of the killer I interviewed as someone who could have been some guy at a bar yelling at the TV screen during a Bears' game. Or Samuel Little. Or Joanna Dennehy. Or any of a list of potential demographics, identifiers or images.

My feeling is that the concept of the "serial murderer," in its definition, is a living organism that changes and grows over the decades, and not only aims to sell to the lowest common denominator but attempts to shape society's thoughts and determine what's considered "normal." This shaping is a cottage industry into itself.

A CHAT WITH A PRODUCER

While on the topic of the media and pop culture and how it intersects with serial murder, I had the occasion to speak with serial killer documentary producer extraordinaire John Borowski, and asked him a few questions:

What do you think of the current popularity of the genre of serial murder within entertainment, such as films, documentaries, Netflix and cable TV? How is it different now than in years prior (or is it?)

Crime has always been a fascinating topic to the public. One of the first reels of films ever shot depicted a cowboy aiming his pistol at the audience and firing. Everyone in the theater ducked when it first screened. Even as a silent film! People not only want to read about true crime, they want to watch it. Documentaries, feature films, mini-series, and television shows based on true crime have always been around and have always been popular. When the Netflix show Mindhunter was released, it seemed to usher in tremendous interest in serial killers and the "mindhunters" that profile them. There has been more released on the subject of serial killers recently, but that may also be due to the proliferation of streaming channels available. All of the "golden age" serial killers have been given new mini-series and films. But how can all this murder be a good thing? If young people can become interested in the fields of psychology, law enforcement, the judicial system, and other scientific and behavioral fields, then they may become our future Albrechts and Hachmeisters or our Douglases and Resslers.

As a filmmaker, do you feel any responsibility or connection for the creation of serial killers as public heroes or entertainment?

I am not responsible just as much as I do not accept responsibility for mankind's interest in true crime. When history is studied, proof of interest in death and crime can be seen as far back as writing began. I am fascinated with the psychology of the serial killer but I am also interested in the historical and sociological aspects of their crimes and the times they lived in. I look at them from a more studio's point of view, even though I feel I create "edutainment" in the visual works I create. I was once called a "folklorist" and I gladly accept that title as I am shining light on truth, it just so happens that my interest is in true crime so I document the people and cases. Serial Killer Culture is still popular but recently I have noticed a few items being created by others that I feel are exploitative. In the past there have been some T-Shirts and other items which featured the serial killer, but I feel some I have recently seen are exploitative and distasteful towards the victims. No one will finish any of my works and cheer. The biographical film works I produce are deep, introspective studies of the serial killers and their crimes.

How do you react to a new generation of young fans being created by recent films featuring extreme murderers like Ted Bundy played by popular actors such as Zac Efron?

I am often invited as a special guest to conventions. Sometimes parents come up to my booth and tell me they are worried about their child and that they are "way too into this stuff." My reaction to them is: Good! If a child can become interested in any field that can stop or incarcerate future murderers, then that is a good thing. We need more young minds interested in the true crime field so that hopefully one day we can figure out the "why." But we may never figure it out. I do find it ironic that several former Disney actors played Dahmer and Bundy.

As an established, prolific filmmaker of movies dealing with the serial killer genre, do you think you look at producing these films in a different light than those making them with no prior experience or with little personal interest?

After producing films for over twenty years I have come to realize that I enjoy creating my works on my own. At least as much as I can do with myself and my equipment. It is difficult to walk the tightrope of business owner and artist. Producing films on Holmes, Fish and Panzram were not as stressful as producing my mini-series on Gacy. What is the key difference? Gacy is still contemporary whereas the other cases have long been closed. While I began producing my Gacy series, the case was still open. So, changes were still happening as far as the unidentified victims and other conspiracy theories. It is difficult for me to comment about others, but I do know that I am now, more than ever, even more interested in finding the ultimate truths in these serial killer/true crime cases and telling their stories as truthfully and interesting as I can. My next film will be about a serial killer with as few victims possible as studying the Gacy case, with 33 victims was like an archival dig for the truth!

An observation has been made that it seems the topic of mass murder is more current and topical today, yet Netflix et al clearly has more material devoted to serial murder. Why do you think that is?

Mass murder is not as interesting as serial murder. What happens in an instant is tragic. What happens over time is frightening. My background of watching horror films was the springboard for my initial interest in serial killers. The appeal to the public lies with psychology, history, crime detection, forensics/lack of and so much more. These can all apply to mass murder stories if the story is told well. There is something to say about the stories of the savage predator getting away with it over time and fooling their own contemporary public and law enforcement. But don't forget about the categories: Lust murderers, vampires, cannibals, killer clown, the list goes on and on…

You have produced documentaries such as the film Serial Killer Culture, which deals with the place of murderabilia within pop culture. Looking back, do you have any opinion of how this topic is viewed today? Has it changed? More/less accepted?

Rick Staton spoke about his being Gacy's art dealer, but the majority of the film was based on serial killers featured in pop culture such as comic books, paintings, songs, etc. I don't hear much about murderabilia nowadays other than people who I know of and are currently in the murderabilia business. I know it definitely isn't big money on a small or individual scale. I would think it is still generally frowned upon. Pogo the clown has become a pop culture reference to John Wayne Gacy but Pogo is almost a pop culture figure himself now. Several people involved in the Gacy case turned me down for interviews after they saw my poster featured Pogo the clown, most likely thinking I am glorifying Gacy, which I am not. I just know how to market my projects.

Tell me your opinion of the idea that the social status quo of a time period helping to create a serial killer such as John Wayne Gacy.

The creation of John Wayne Gacy as a serial killer was a perfect storm. His adolescence was in 1950's America. The worst time for gays in the history of the country. Being gay was illegal. So Gacy had to hide his homosexual feelings. He repressed those feelings for years and they first came out as rape and attempted murder, which blossomed into becoming a serial killer. Gacy hid his victims in his crawlspace, just as he had hidden his homosexuality for so long. (Related to above)

A current sensation is the film, Joker. Do you see any kernel of truth to the message, "you get what you fucking deserve?"

I can see how society can create monsters. H.H. Holmes was the product of the gilded age, Albert Fish took the Bible literally, Gacy was created by hatred and homophobia. Are we learning any lessons? Many times I return to the writings of Carl Panzram and wonder if he was right on some things…and I don't mean might.

(AUTHOR NOTE): Panzram was one of the greatest examples of a killer who was produced by society, a monster who exemplified the concept of "you get what you deserve." One of his famous quotes was, "This lesson I was taught by others: Might makes right."

REFERENCES

Aamodt, Michael. (2020). *Radford/FGCU annual report on serial killer statistics: 2020.*

Aamodt, Fox, Hickey, Hinch, Labuschagne, Levin, McClellan, Nelson, Newton, Quinet, Steiger, White, & Yaksic. (2021). *Consolidated Serial Homicide Offender Database.* Harvard Dataverse. https://dataverse.harvard.edu/dataverse/serial_homicide.

Adjorlolo & Chan (2014). The controversy of defining serial murder: Revisited. *Journal of Aggression and Violent Behavior.* 19 (5). DOI: 10.1016/j.avb.2014.07.003.

American Psychiatric Association. (2013). *Diagnostic and statistical manual of mental disorders, 5th edition.* Arlington, VA: American Psychiatric Publishing. (Also references to 3rd and 4th editions).

Arias, Pilar. (2021, December 20). 4th alleged shopping cart killer victim could be missing woman from California. *Fox News/MSN.com.* wwwfoxnews.com.

Backderf, Derf. (2012). *My friend Dahmer.* New York, NY. Abrams ComicArts.

Branson, Allan. (2013). African American serial killers, over-represented yet underacknowledged. *The Howard Journal of Criminal Justice.* Vol 52, Issue 1, pp 1-18.

Copycat. (1995). Regency Enterprises. Warner Bros.

Delisio, Meredith. (2022, January 8). 5th victim possibly linked to 'shopping cart killer,' as policy identify 2 others. *ABC News.* abcnews.go.com.

Douthwaite, L.C. (1929). *Mass murder.* New York, NY. Henry Holt and Company, Inc.

Egger, Steven (1990). *Serial murder: An elusive phenomenon.* Westport, CT. Praeger.

Egger, Steven. (1997, 2002). *The killers among us. 1st & 2nd Ed. An examination of serial murder and its investigation.* Upper Saddle River, NJ. Pearson Education/Prentice-Hall.

Federal Bureau of Investigation; Behavioral Analysis Unit-2. (2008). *Serial Murder: Multi-disciplinary perspectives for investigators.* 2005 Symposium report. National Center for the Analysis of Violent crime.

Fox, Levin & Fridel. (2019). *Extreme killing, 4th Ed.* Los Angeles, CA. Sage Publications.

Friedel, E.E. & Fox, J.A. (2018). Too few victims: Finding the optimal minimum victim threshold for defining serial murder. *Psychology of Violence,* 8(4), 505-514 DOI: 10.1037/vio0000138.

Hickey, Eric. (2016). *Serial murderers and their victims,* 7th Ed. Boston, MA. Cengage Learning.

Jenkins, Phillip. (1993). African-Americans and serial homicide. *American Journal of*

Criminal Justice, Vol 17 47-60. DOI: 10.1007/BF02885953.

Safarik, M. & Ramsland, K. (2020). *Spree Killers: Practical classifications for law enforcement and criminology.* New York, NY, CRC Press.

Shanafelt & Pino. (2013). Evil and the common life: Towards a wider perspective on serial killing and atrocities. *New Directions in Crime and Deviancy.* Routledge.

Yaksic, Enzo. (2006). *Can a demographic make you psychopathic?* (presentation/article).

Yaksic, Enzo. (2015). Addressing the challenges and limitations of utilizing data to study serial homicide. *Crime Psychology Review.* 1(1): 108-134.

Yaksic, Enzo. (2018). The folly of counting bodies: Using regression to transgress the state of serial murder classification systems. *Aggression and Violent Behavior*, Vol 43, Nov-Dec, 26-32. DOI: 10.1016/j.avb.2018.08.007.

Yaksic, Allely, De Silva, Smith-Inglis, Konikoff, Ryan, Gordon, Denisov & Keatley. (2019). Detecting a decline in serial homicide: Have we banished the devil from the details? *Cogent Social Sciences*, 5:1. DOI: 10.1080/23311886.2019.1678450.

Yaksic, Harrison, Konikoff, Mooney, Allely, De Silva, Matykiewicz, Inglis, Giannangelo, Daniels, Sarteschi. (2021). A heuristic study of the similarities and differences in offender characteristics across potential and successful serial sexual homicide offenders. *Behavioral Sciences and the Law.* 39(1). DOI 10.1002/bsl.2510.

Yaksic, Enzo. (2022). *Killer data. Modern perspectives on serial murder.* Oxfordshire, England, UK. Routledge/Taylor and Francis Group.

Wolfe, Molly. (2020, August 31). Serial Killers are fascinating- except when they're black. *ShoutoutUK.*

World Health Organization (WHO). (2019). *International statistical classification of diseases and related health problems (ICD-10). 10th revision.* World Health Organization.

CHAPTER 7

What if Child Pornography wasn't illegal?
Miyazaki had to kill to break the law.

"I felt so alone. And whenever I saw a little girl playing on her own, it was almost like seeing myself."

-Tsutomu Miyazaki

Frankly, sometimes I feel like I've heard it all. After teaching Psychology of the Offender and Serial Murder for over 20 years, I've read most of the topics I'd expect on a research paper. But in 2017, Amanda Mullin, one of my students, brought me a name I hadn't heard of: Tsutomu Miyazaki. AKA, The Otaku Murderer.

Miyazaki was a Japanese cannibal and a necrophile who abducted and killed 4 young girls in Saitama and Toyo between August 1988 and June 1989. He was also accused of vampirism. He preserved body parts of victims as trophies.

Miyazaki, after his arrest, attempted an unsuccessful insanity defense in an effort to save his life. He came up with the clever moniker "The Rat Man" for his psychological alter-ego and blamed him for his crimes. However, it would be to no avail as 11 years after his conviction, he was hanged for his sordid acts of torture and murder.

BACKGROUND

Tsutomu Miyazaki was born in 1962 in Itsukaichi, Tokyo, Japan. He suffered with a birth defect: deformed hands, which were permanently gnarled and fused directly to the wrists, resulting in having to move his entire forearm in order to rotate the hand. This condition, congenital radioulnar fusion disease, reportedly resulted from premature birth. However, later it was discovered that he was not the biological child of his mother but born out of an incestuous relationship between his father and his sister. This suggested a far more insidious origin to his birth defect. Some felt this was just a story to explain Miyazaki's horrible deeds; others felt it was all too shameful, in a culture who is extra-sensitive to such matters, to be a lie.

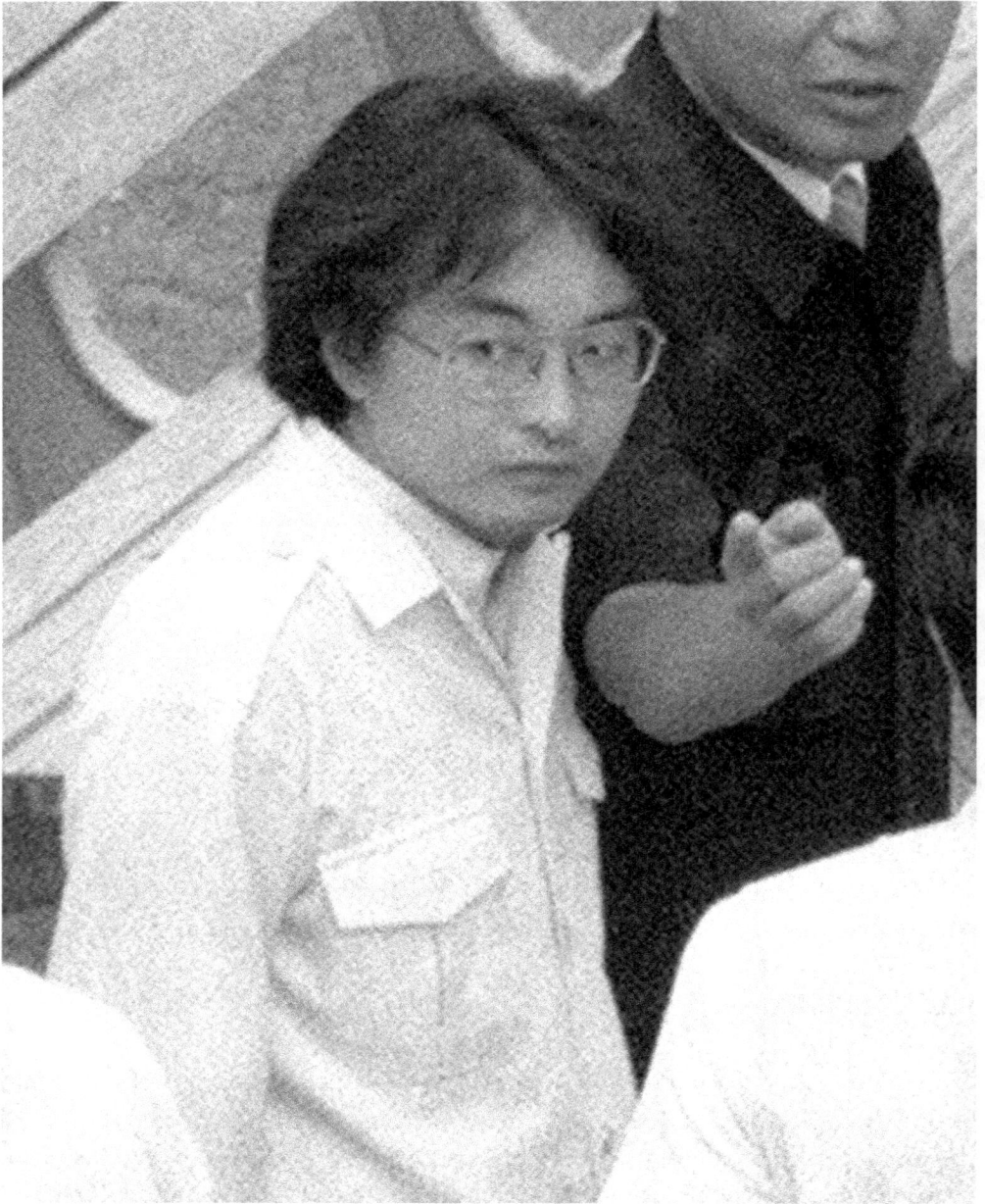

Tsutomu Miyazaki, Tokyo, Japan 1989. (AP Photo/Kyodo News.)

He was cruelly bullied due to his deformed hands in school. This is an obvious potential factor in his warped personality development and anger. His parents, who were relatively well-off for the times, put an enormous amount of pressure on him regarding his grades. He was an excellent student at first, but this declined over time. His original plan to become an English teacher was eventually replaced by being trained to become a photo technician as his poor grades hurt his entry to his preferred school, Meiji University. Instead, he attended Junior College.

As a child, he was rejected by his younger sisters, Setsuko and Haruko, as well as his peers and was not close to his parents who did not want to hear about his problems which included thoughts of suicide. He was reportedly very close to a grandfather who seemed to be the only person with which he had a connection. Miyazaki grew despondent and depressed after his grandfather's sudden death. He reportedly ate parts of his grandfather's ashes, feeling he would "retain something" from him.

Tsutomu exhibited acting-out behaviors before his crimes. He told interviewers he killed cats as a child, tossing them in the river. He reportedly tortured another by dropping it in boiling water.

Miyazaki, who was supposedly obsessed with and influenced by Japanese anime and pornography, was caught a few weeks after his grandfather's death by one of his sisters, watching her as she was taking a shower. She told him to leave, and he responded by attacking her. When his mother heard about what happened, she reprimanded him and he then attacked her, too. His mother kicked him out of the house, telling him to get a job.

Some of his other behaviors included silent harassing phone calls made to families of future victims Miyazaki had selected. Miyazaki would breathe heavily into the phone and nothing else. He would call over and over if the calls were not answered, letting the phone ring constantly for nearly a half-hour at a time.

A few weeks after the incident with his sister and mother, Tsutomu Miyazaki progressed to murder.

HIS CRIMES

The Victims:

Mari Konno

Tsutomu Miyazaki's first murder was of a four-year-old girl named Mari Konno. On

August 22, 1988, she was abducted and strangled by Tsutomu just outside Tokyo after disappearing while playing at a friend's house. He reverted to his photography training, taking pictures of Konno's body, which was sexually abused post-mortem. Like many serial killers he collected trophies by keeping her clothes and escalated later by returning to the corpse and cutting off her feet and hands, keeping them in his closet and found later and returned to her family. Her parents worried that Mari could not walk and eat in Heaven without her feet and hands.

Days after her disappearance, an anonymous postcard was received by her parents stating, "there are devils about." A package was sent to her family that contained her shorts, underwear, sandals, charred crushed bone fragments and 10 baby teeth along with a letter with words cut from the newspaper that said, "Mari. Cremated. Bones. Investigate. Prove."

Days after the package was received, a letter titled, "Crime Confession" was sent to Mari's mother, confessing to the murder in total, stating "I did everything" and explaining he was concerned that the mother was holding out hope for her survival and return. A final letter was tauntingly sent to the family describing the corpse's rigidity, skin and coloring and commenting "… and it smells. How it smells."

(NOTE: some accounts seem to have minor detail differences in them regarding the crimes, such as whether Mari's clothes or photos of her clothes were sent to the parents. In all the accounts of the crimes, there have been minor detail variances. This may be a translation issue or something else, but the crime detail differences I found were insignificant.)

Masami Yoshizawa

Next was 7-year-old Masami Yoshizawa, killed on October 3, 1988. He spotted her while she was walking along the road headed home after her first-grade class and offered her a ride in his Nissan. He took Masami to the same place where he committed his first crime, a wooded area, and strangled her. Post-mortem, Yoshizawa was mutilated, sexually abused, and left in the same general area as Konno. He took her clothes as trophies as well.

Erika Namba

Victim #3 was Erika Namba, age 4, kidnapped on December 12, 1988, while walking home from a friend's house. He took her to a parking lot in Naguri, Saitama and forced her to remove her clothes. He and took several photos of her before killing her. He strangled her to stop her from sobbing. He tied her hands and feet behind her back after the murder. For some reason he did not keep her clothes. He got a wheel on his car stuck on his way to dispose of the body and dumped it in a wooded area nearby. A couple strangers later helped him move his car but did not witness the disposal. The body was quickly found afterward. A week later, the Namba family received a postcard with Japanese kanji words cut out of magazines that read, "Erika. Cold. Cough. Throat. Rest. Death."

Ayako Nomoto

His fourth and final victim was five-year-old Ayako Nomoto on June 6, 1989. In this case he convinced her to let him take pictures of her in his car after finding her playing at a park. Unfortunately for Ayako, she commented on Miyazaki's deformed hands, and he flew into a rage, killing her. He beat and strangled her, saying, "this is what happens to kids who say things like that!" After stopping in the town of Koenji to rent a camera, he took the body to his apartment to photograph and film, including incredibly graphic photos of Nomoto's vagina taped open.

He masturbated on the body and committed necrophilia for two days. Later he dismembered the corpse, hid the torso in a cemetery and tossed the head in the hills nearby. He kept the hands and feet and committed cannibalism for the first time, eating parts of them as well as drinking her blood. He later returned to the cemetery and the hills, fearing the authorities would find her remains. He carried them back to his apartment where he hid them in his closet.

ARREST AND TRIAL

When Tsutomu Miyazaki was trying to take nude pictures of a girl on July 23, 1989, attempting to insert a zoom lens into her vagina, he was confronted by her father who immediately called the Police. The victim's sister had escaped the assault and ran home to get her father. When Miyazaki, who had fled naked from the scene, returned to retrieve his car, he was arrested. (Another detailed version of this segment has the father beating Miyazaki and handing him directly to Police.) The Police searched his house and found video footage and pictures of his victims. Miyazaki remained indifferent after his capture and showed no remorse.

The media named him 'the Otaku Murderer' due to his obsession with anime. A search of his home resulted in the discovery of almost 6000 videotapes including anime and slasher films. Some were the Guinea Pig slasher series dealing in realistic special effects in torture and murder. Also included were videos of his siblings showering and his victims in pornographic poses. His collection of pornography and violence was also blamed for adding to his perversion and crimes. His father was ashamed of his actions and refused to pay for his son's legal defense. He eventually committed suicide.

As in many violent crimes, some in the public jumped on the bandwagon of blaming anime, horror films and otaku in general for the violence. Other public comments included claims that the collection of pornography was planted later and, also some accused the release of this information was strategy to stoke a public reaction that would ensure a conviction.

During his trial, Miyazaki talked nonsensically and blamed his alter ego the 'Rat Man' for forcing him to commit the murders. A diminished capacity defense was his only hope, of course. He also justified his killings saying they were 'acts of benevolence'. Not only did he not display any remorse, but he also actually felt proud of himself and his deeds. At one point he asserted that he would be acquitted and that "I don't intend on apologizing."

Despite many attempts to label him as insane, he was judged as aware of the magnitude and consequences of his crimes, and he was sentenced to death in April 1997. His death sentence was upheld by the Tokyo High Court and later by the Supreme Court of Justice. He was hanged on June 17, 2008.

OTAKU, ANIME AND MANGA

Miyazaki's identification as "The Otaku Murderer" is an interesting point. At the time of the crimes, the culture used the term, "Otaku" as a term of derision and scorn. It essentially described a slacker who had no ambition, no interest in growing up or succeeding as an adult, and immersing himself in a life of video games, anime, and comic books. A typical Otaku would be a lazy recluse, masturbating to comic books, not terribly unlike Miyazaki. These days, there's a counterculture that celebrates this cool, quirky "lifestyle choice" and identifies themselves as "Otaku" with pride. As in many cases, the current, common use of a term's concept bears little resemblance to its initial intent.

Otaku is a Japanese derogatory term for people with obsessive interests, particularly in anime and manga. Its contemporary use originated with Akio Nakamori's 1983 essay in Manga Burikko. **Otaku** may be used as a pejorative; its negativity stems from a stereotypical view of **otaku** and the media's reporting on Tsutomu Miyazaki.

Anime is hand-drawn and computer animations originating from or associated with Japan. The word anime is the Japanese word for animation, which means all forms of animated media. It's always had its detractors, with some reports of a 1997 Pokemon cartoon sending children to the hospital due to a 20 second strobe effect. Other complaints about sex and violence and glorifying crime have been voiced along with the appreciation of the art, graphics, and creative storytelling.

Manga are comics or graphic novels created in Japan or are Japanese-related, conforming to a style developed in Japan in the late 19th Century. The word references both comics and cartooning.

Loli hentai is a form of the pornographic sexualization of children in the above images.

An anime image: "Winter School girl." (Maxwindy/Shutterstock.)

CHILD PORNOGRAPHY… WAS NOT ILLEGAL?

An underlying storyline in the Miyazaki case is the fact that at the time, owning child pornography was not illegal. Worse, the Japanese culture appeared to have little urgency or interest in making it against the law. Whether it was too lucrative a business for a great many people or there were far too many "mainstream" individuals interested in child porn, this was a fact of the culture of the day.

For context, this was also a culture that allowed cannibal murderer and necrophile Issei Sagawa to check himself out of the Matsuzawa Psychiatric Hospital in Tokyo in 1986. After murdering and devouring his friend Renee Hartevelt in Paris, he was deported to Japan where he was supposed to spend the rest of his life in a Japanese mental hospital. However, the system was so flawed that the court documents were sealed, ending the criminal case against Sagawa. He walked away from the hospital and has led a life of infamy and celebrity to this day. For the record, Sagawa says he plans to eat human flesh again before he dies.

In 1984 at the age of 21, Miyazaki began to watch child pornography, which was legal at that time. In 2014, Japan finally banned child pornography. Under the new law, people found with explicit photos or video of children could be imprisoned for up to one year and fined up to 1 million yen ($10,000). The passage of the legislation came after years of international pressure urging laws against the possession of child pornography, which activists said endangered children. Despite banning the production and distribution of child pornography in 1999, Japan was the last major nation to make possession a punishable offense. People also had a 1-year grace period to get rid of the illegal materials. Apparently, the urgency was still not taken seriously.

Japan was known as an "international hub for the production and trafficking of child pornography," according to the 2013 U.S. Department of State's human-rights report. In 2012, the Police reported investigations involving 1,264 child victims featured in pornography — a 98% increase from the previous year.

Still, the new law did not include the banning of anime and manga that feature explicit scenes of children, after lawyers and publishers argued that censoring the materials would curb free speech. A lawyer for the Japan Animation Creators Association told CNN that the new law was to protect children from abuse and that banning animation "would not satisfy the goal of the law." It was thought that Manga (comic depictions) of children were "not real children." What was reality was that it was too profitable. Another subject is the concept of "loli" or "loli hentai" which is the apparent sexualization of young children within anime or anime pornography. People have continued to complain about this issue.

Politicians said the 2014 law intended to change the cultural acceptance of child por-

"The background of beautiful anime girl shaped cats." (kirigaya_project/Shutterstock).

nography fighting against a tendency of looking at children as sexual objects, and allowing them to be taken advantage of, sexually and commercially. The idea that direct correlation between child pornography and abuse is unmistakable. Were the thousands of victims who were forced to create the child porn considered to be legally possessed not a factor? Were they willing participants? Unlikely.

Of course, child sexual assault and abuse was not legal at any point in time. But seriously, does a culture that does not reject child pornography create an environment where sexual use of a child is a natural byproduct? And even after laws are instituted, there's still a level of legality within anime, which was the main purview of Tsutomu Miyazaki. As in most conversations about pornography and their effects, do violent pedophiles like Miyazaki seek out anime that features underaged sexualized subjects… or is his existence a result caused by them? What do you think?

At any rate, Miyazaki's crimes seemed to be those of violence and murder, although his victims' families would argue they did in fact begin with rape and quite possibly, fueled by the very legal ownership and viewing of child pornography.

REFERENCES

Defendant admits abducting and killing schoolgirl in Nara. (2005, April 19). *The Japan Times*. Kyodo News. www.japantimes.co.jp.

Hellmann, Melissa. (2014, June 18). Japan finally bans child pornography. *Time*. https://time.com.

Miyazaki unrepentant to the last/ Serial child killer goes to execution without apologizing or explaining his thinking. (2008, June 18). *The Yomiuri Shimbun*. Narkive Newsgroup Archive. alt.obituaries.narkive.com.

Mullin, Amanda. (2017). *Tsutomu Miyazaki- Research paper*. University of Illinois Springfield.

Serena, Katie. (2021). Cannibal killer Issei Sagawa is walking free and plans to eat humans again. *Allthatsinteresting.com*.

The horrific Japanese serial murders of cannibal Tsutomu Miyazaki. (2020, July 25). *Talk murder to me*. https://talkmurder.com.

Turner, Joe. (2021, June 16). The myth of Tsutomu Miyazaki's hands. *Joe Turner* (blog). www.joeturnerbooks.com.

Welton, Benjamin. (2015, February 8). Japanese psycho: Tsutomu Miyazaki, the otaku murderer. *The Trebuchet*. Literary Trebuchet Blogspot.

Whipple, Charles T. (2007, August 18). The silencing of the lambs. *Charlest.whipple.net*.

CHAPTER 8

The Lady… Killers. Different? They Used to Be.
Female serial killers seem to be evolving with the times.

"That is my ambition, to have killed more people… helpless
people… than any man or woman who has ever lived."
-Jane Toppan

Studying women serial killers has always been a challenge.

It's always been hard enough to construct a working definition of what the serial killer is. That's always been a goal, defining the elements of the serial murderer. The typology. The personality and behavioral characteristics.

Then you add gender, and everything goes out the window.

Seemed that serial killers, usually men, committed lust killings. They preferred to kill hands-on. Their killings did not generally appear to be motivated by financial gain. Their victims were of a consistent gender. They were rarely considered insane.

Female serial killer cases defied all these conventions.

SERIAL KILLER WOMEN IN HISTORY

Over multiple decades, Norwegian Belle Gunness killed anywhere between 25-40 people in Illinois and Indiana, culminating in 1908. She murdered them mainly for valuables and insurance. Gunness' run came to a spectacular end when she reportedly faked her own death in a fire, leaving behind a headless corpse.

Jane Toppan, the Boston female killer known as "Jolly Jane," confessed to 31 murders in 1901, was suspected of over 100, and managed to avoid criminal responsibility by being found not guilty by reason of insanity. This appeared to work against her as she was committed for life rather than having a chance for release. This "Angel of Death" typology serial murderer was known to hold her victims close after poisoning them and reveled in the intimate control she experienced. She reportedly got a powerful erotic charge from caressing them as they lay dying.

Between the 1920s and 1950s, Nannie Doss murdered between 8-11 victims in multiple states. They consisted of family members and husbands. For insurance money. The "Giggling Granny" finally confessed after the death of her 5th husband.

In the 70s and 80s, Marybeth Tinning suspiciously suffered the loss of 8 of her nine children, one at a time. She blamed the deaths on sudden infant death syndrome (SIDS). She reportedly enjoyed the attention. Later, she said she just started killing her children after she lost her first to acute spinal meningitis. Marybeth was also in the process of poisoning her husband. She was paroled in 2018.

Beverly Allitt, a UK nurse, received 13 life sentences in 1993 after being convicted of the murders of 4 children and the attempts to murder 9 more in her care at a hospital children's ward. Allitt is also to be considered for parole soon.

Another Angel of Death nurse, Kristen Gilbert in the mid-1990s, was thought to have been responsible for 80-350 deaths and 300 assaults in a Massachusetts VA hospital from injections of epinephrine, resulting in patients who needed to be resuscitated after cardiac arrests. It's thought many were to gain attention and praise from her hospital security/Police boyfriend. She also dodged a potential death sentence after a conviction of 4 murders.

Gilbert's and Allitt's glory-seeking behaviors could also be viewed as similar to those individuals with Munchausen Syndrome by Proxy, another condition associated with female serial killers. Tinning's crimes are often linked with Munchausen as well.

ASSUMPTIONS AND STEREOTYPES

Who are these women? They are examples of what we have thought of when we consider the female serial killer. Hard to believe they did it. Hard to catch. Often getting away with their crimes for much longer than they should. Easily considered insane and rarely executed. And at the very least, any observer would note that some of these heinous crimes were not punished as you might expect a male offender would. Some of the cases end in parole.

They also seemed to fall into similar motivational categories: Murders for money. Insurance. Often killing husbands or family. Or babies. Suffering from Munchausen syndrome by proxy or another mental illness. Or functioning as real-life Angels of Death, executing scores of victims within a hospital or medical setting.

Female "team" killers seemed to be somewhat consistent in their actions... pleasing their mates or partners but unwillingly operating under duress. Or at least trying to make that case at trial. Karla Homolka was last seen quietly living in Quebec after raping and murdering 3 (including her little sister) with her husband and serving a short prison term due to a plea deal publicly reviled as a gift rather than an appropriate punishment. Caril Ann Fugate, however, unsuccessfully tried to blame her boyfriend Charles Starkweather for her role in their 10 spree murders and received a life sentence. More than one female team killer who seemed more than enthusiastic in participating in the crimes suddenly developed a coerced victim status post-capture.

Caril Fugate and Charles Starkweather. (1959, Uncredited/AP/Shutterstock.)

This is the stuff movies are made of. And long-held stereotypes.

Then Aileen Wuornos sauntered into our consciousness. The homicidal prostitute lured targeted men into vulnerable situations and killed them with no warning, shooting them at close range. Is this a new kind of killer? Predictably, some tried to excuse away her behavior as an understandable reaction to abusive clients. People questioned the very existence of female serial killers when the story went national in the early 90s. But we knew better.

It was possible Aileen was a different kind of lady killer. She did seem to be a more active, aggressive, hands-on predator than what we were used to. She did seem to truly dislike the men she murdered and was acting out of a long-held rage, possibly suffering from Intermittent Explosive Disorder. But on the other hand, she was routinely stealing money and personal items for her girlfriend Ty all along. So maybe she wasn't that different from the prototypical female serial murderer after all.

Wuornos did wander into male killers' territory in one important way: she was actually executed for her crimes in 2002.

THE MURDEROUS WOMEN OF TODAY

These days, we still have plenty of stories about females with Munchausen, putting their children at risk of death for attention and profit. There're still stories about Angels of Death… Canadian Elly Mae Westlaufer was one, who commented on an unexplainable need to kill with a childlike explanation: "it seems all so stupid now. I'm so embarrassed." She confessed to the murders of 8 senior citizens and 7 other attempts after her arrest in 2016.

To be fair, there's been plenty of male Angels of Death in medical settings.

But it does look as if the women of today have taken the next step. Consider:

Daniella Poggiali, after a few rounds in the Italian court system, was finally convicted of murder for repeated executions of elderly patients in her care as a nurse. She received a sentence of 30 years in 2020. It seems her disregard for human life wasn't much different than Gilbert's who was known to ask if she could get off early if one of her patients died. But Poggiali took on a modern twist when she decided to *pose for selfies* with the corpses of recently deceased patients, complete with goofy mugging for the camera.

Another woman displaying new characteristics was Johanna Dennehy, the architect of the Peterborough (England) Ditch Murders. Over a 2-week period, she stabbed to death 2 of her housemates and her landlord. With the help of male minions (another oddity for the female killer) dumped the bodies in ditches and later attempted to stab strangers to death in broad daylight.

Joanna Dennehy. (2013, London, Britain. Geoffrey Robinson/Shutterstock.)

Dennehy said she "killed to see if I was as cold as I thought I was" and then got a taste for it. She attempted to continue to "have her fun" while she was being investigated. She also posed at least one of the bodies sexually, after being clad in a black sequin dress. Significant, different behaviors? Seems so.

She was given a life sentence (a "whole-life tariff") in 2014.

Elena Lobacheva, AKA the "Bride of Chucky," also represents the new breed in female serial killer. The Russian-born killer took part in murders with a gang of roving attackers who murdered homeless men on the street. Lobacheva helped to butcher 14, stabbing and using a hammer on them in an attempt to clean the Moscow streets of vagrants.

She told Police that "randomly stabbing the body of a dying human brought her pleasure compared to sexual pleasure."

Lobacheva said that she "enjoyed killing" and the attacks were so violent, parts of one victim's brain were found 16 feet away from the body.

She also professed a hero-worship of Russian serial killer Alexander Picushkin, who killed 49 people.

Seems there's still benefits to gender: she received a sentence of only 13 years in 2017.

Lobacheva wasn't the only woman now emulating the exploits of a male serial murderer. Another Russian, Tamara Samsonova, known as "The Granny Ripper," was reportedly obsessed with the horrific crimes of the terrifying Soviet serial killer Andrei Chikatilo. Samsonova, who confessed to 11 murders in her diary also admitted to cutting up victims into pieces to dispose of them and eating parts of the bodies, like her hero Chikatilo. She reportedly killed over a period of 21 years and was arrested in 2015.

Today we have a potential new serial killer team couple in the U.S. Lori Vallow and her husband Chad Daybell, who are charged with the murders of Vallow's 2 children and conspiracy in the executions of both couple's previous spouses and possibly her brother. The bodies of Vallow's children were found buried in Daybell's back yard after they seemingly vanished for months.

Daybell, a professional gravedigger turned doomsday novelist, developed extreme religious beliefs of the impending end of the world. Vallow, a fan of Daybell's whose interest developed into a cult-like obsession, reportedly believed she was chosen by God to carry out His mission of the apocalypse. She also felt part of her mission, as a god, was to eliminate the darkness, the "zombies," the demonic and the evil. These included her husband and eventually her children. Vallow's brother, who shot Vallow's husband also died mysteriously, as did Daybell's wife.

Each person's specific roles in the deaths are still unclear, but Lori Vallow's participation in several people's deaths, including her 2 children, remains a strong possibility as the ticket to her future label as a modern female serial killer or team killer.

And very recently, Chinese female/team serial killer Lao Rongzhi, after 20 years on the run, was sentenced to death for her active participation in 7 murders which included a 3-year-old. Unsurprisingly, she blamed her boyfriend for forcing her to help kill. He was executed in 1999.

So, in recent years, female killers have taken on many new characteristics. Posing for selfies with dead bodies. Describing sexual pleasure in stabbing people to death. Enlisting male surrogates. Posing and dressing up corpses. Gleefully describing the enjoyment of murder with a dismissive absence of remorse or empathy. Murdering children. Aggressive violent hands-on personal attacks. Engaging in cannibalism. Hero worship of famous male serial murderers. Maybe even doomsday plots and systematic executions of their husband and children.

The prototypical female killers of hospital patients due to mental illness, babies for attention and husbands for insurance money have evolved. The clear-cut gender differences between the male and female serial killers of the past are feeling more like a memory. The study of serial murder is unlikely to ever be the same.

(Parts of this section originally printed in *Serial Killer Magazine*, 2021)

THE STUDY OF FEMALE SERIAL KILLERS

In both of my previous books, I've pointed to the study of female serial killers to be an aspect of this genre that needs an extensive expansion. We are progressing from the days where female serial killers were simply a contradiction and a mystery, and I hope analysis is becoming more expansive and with greater depth.

However, thorough texts like Peter Vronsky's *Female Serial Killers*, which examines the topic as specifically as possible, are few and far between. The fact is that some of the stereotypes about female killers remain. And it's true that the depth of the histories and psychological background analysis in female serial killer cases can seem lacking, possibly due to lower numbers, maybe because of glossing over details. But there's interesting histories like that of the Mexican female serial murderer Juana Barraza, who blamed her kills both on a broken society that caused her economic strife as well as a motivation that included disdain for elderly women, much like the mother who bitterly failed her throughout her life. These cases need to be looked at more closely.

Earlier in this chapter I've touched on some of the differences in female behavior in recent cases, behavior that mirrors more of male serial killers. I've had several female students point out that one of the problems in the study of females seems to be that this research is always in context with males. While I agree this is a rut that can get a researcher stuck, it is relevant and a reasonable teaching point. I'd like to move away from men as suggested and look at women as their own topic. However, it seems when analyzing women as a specific subset of serial murders, it often feels incomplete to not point out the things that make them both different and similar to the other 90% or so of the killer population. So, I'm very open for suggestions as to how to properly research women without using the context of male killers as a comparison.

Another point made by students is the analysis of females is terribly thin when it comes to both social and psychological histories. It's been noted that historically, women are more easily considered legally insane, possibly because of the way this fits into the narrative that it's just harder to accept women as dangerous and homicidal. It also fits a narrative that women kill over emotion (or money) as opposed to men who kill for sex.

Let's be reasonable in our context… according to the 2020 Radford Database, women have comprised approximately 8.6 % of total U.S. serial killers for decades now. This is consistent with homicide in general… men vastly commit more homicides (and most crime overall) than women. So "underestimating" women as dangerous and murderous is reasonable… women simply commit these types of crimes less often. However, once we acknowledge this, we should also acknowledge that the women that DO decide to kill are every bit as dangerous, violent, and deadly as their male counterparts, and often more so.

A FEMALE HANNIBAL LECTER?

Look at Katherine Mary Knight of Australia. In 2000 the talented meatworker decided she'd had enough of her partner John Price and chased him around his home until she successfully stabbed him 37 times, in the front and back of his body, killing him. This, after taking out a restraining order against her for stabbing him in the chest after a series of assaults during their relationship. That day, Price told his co-workers that if he didn't come to work the next day, it would be because Katherine had murdered him.

But this was just the beginning of her activity. Katherine then proceeded to behead him and then remove his skin from his body, so expertly that it formed a one-piece "pelt" that was able to be re-used and re-attached to his remains for burial. This skin was left hanging on a meat hook on a door frame to the living room.

Not done yet. After posing the body in a degrading position to properly convey her complete disregard for Mr. Price, she cooked parts of his body in a stew with various vegetables, intending to serve it up to her children for dinner.

But let's look back at Knight's past. Her history of violence and aggression was life-long. She never had a relationship with a man that did not include violence and what could be attempted murder.

Her marriage to David Kellett began with Knight's mother warning him on his wedding day that Katherine "would fucking kill you" if he didn't watch out. On their wedding night, Knight tried to strangle Kellett because, as she explained, he'd fallen asleep after only having intercourse three times.

Later in their violent relationship, Knight fractured Kellett's skull with a frying pan and burned his clothing while she was pregnant. After he left her for another woman, she left her two-month-old baby on a train track, stole an axe and threatened several people. Shortly afterwards, she slashed the face of a woman and forced her to drive to find Kellett. She then kidnapped a boy before being apprehended by Police. After being admitted to a psychiatric hospital, she admitted her plan was to kill the mechanic who fixed her husband's car, which enabled him to leave, and then kill her husband and his mother. In an odd reaction to this news, her husband left his new girlfriend and returned to take care of Knight, along with his mother.

In another relationship, she cut the throat of a two-month-old dingo pup belonging to a man with whom she had an on and off again relationship, as a threat regarding any thought of an affair. She followed this up by knocking him unconscious with a frying pan, apparently a favorite weapon of Miss Katherine's. On another occasion she hit him in the face with an iron and stabbed him in the abdomen with scissors. The man, David Saunders, eventually went into hiding to escape Knight and later was served with an Apprehended Violence Order after she lied to Police about him threatening Knight and their child.

Her early history is also interesting. Her mother, who was forced to move away from her husband and 4 sons due to an adulterous relationship moved Katherine and 3 additional children into her new lover's home. Her mother was reportedly raped up to 10 times a day by Katherine's violent, alcoholic, and torturous father. Unsurprisingly, her mother despised both men and sex, never failing to pass this perspective onto her daughters. Knight claimed she was repeatedly sexually assaulted by family members up to age 11. She also reported being visited by the ghost of an uncle who committed suicide in 1969. She was a bully towards children and teachers alike in school and left at age 15 without learning to read or write.

Katherine Knight wasn't a serial killer but given her circumstances easily could have been if any of her previous targets had died. She was a violent murderer dubbed "the female Hannibal Lecter" who was as dangerous a monster as could be found. She's also barely known about within the genre.

But she's not without her contemporaries. 24-year-old Taylor Schabusiness of Wisconsin was arrested in March 2022, after allegedly hacking her lover to pieces after choking him to death during a meth-fueled sexual encounter. She left behind a bucket containing his head and genitals. A crock pot box containing additional human body parts including legs along with an upper torso, multiple knives, and body fluid in a container were also found.

Schabusiness stated she blacked out during the encounter and remembered "going crazy" when she began strangling the victim. She said she enjoyed choking the victim, who had a chain around his neck during a sex act. She said she did not intend to kill him but choked him until he died, saying "she was already this far." She was waiting for him to die while watching his face, wanting to see what happens. It's reported she sexually assaulted the victim for 2-3 hours after the murder. When asked what had happened, she reportedly responded, "That is a good question."

She also asked detectives if "they knew what it was like to love something so much that you kill it" and also told Police they "were going to have fun trying to find all the organs."

ANOTHER TEAM YOU'VE NEVER HEARD ABOUT

While we are discussing cases about women killers you may have never heard of, let's move on to a rarely publicized female-male set of team serial killers: David and Catherine Birnie.

One factor when looking at Catherine Birnie specifically in this context is, her personal history is more developed than many female serial murderers or team serial killers. Not to mention there's nothing about her participation in crimes that she could palm off as committing under duress, like many of the Karla Homolkas or Caril Fugates out there.

David John and Catherine Margaret Birnie were a pair of team killers who terrorized Western Australia in 1986 committing the Moorhouse serial killings. They tortured, raped and killed four women and attempted a fifth kill. They were never married, but Catherine, dubbed "The Puppeteer" of the pair, decided to take Birnie's name.

David's history was a sad one. His mother ignored and abandoned David and his four siblings, leaving them to fend for themselves for food, personal hygiene, or anything else for that matter. The home was a den of squalor and filth. His childhood was likely a study in attachment disorder. David's mom was a loud chain-smoking alcoholic who physically and emotionally abused the children. She dominated David's timid physically handicapped father, known for his noticeable stutter.

The kids had to feed themselves throughout the day, sometimes on spoiled food left out.

There were stories of incest between the children and the parents.

Finally, mercifully, David's parents divorced and sent the kids to foster care. At Sunday school he displayed disturbing behavior, damaging things and acting out. He repeated the fifth and eighth grades and at eight years old started committing petty crimes. He was known for exposing himself and harming animals at a racecourse where he worked.

Catherine's young life wasn't any better. Her mother died during childbirth when Catherine was two years old. Her brother died shortly after birth. She was eventually sent to live with her father in South Africa, who sent her to her grandparents in Australia who in turn sent her to different homes. The rejection and lack of bonding was horrible. While with her grandparents, she was not allowed to play with or socialize with other children. Her lack of bonding and socialization was traumatic on Catherine.

David and Catherine met at age 12. David was a dropout at 15 and at 16 attempted to rape a woman in her home. He was addicted to porn and was sexually disturbed already. Both married other people and then they met up again years later. At this time, they discovered their mutual interest in sexual sadism.

Their first crime together was in 1969. They went to a drive-in movie theater and tried to steal a safe. David was sent to prison for almost 4 years while Catherine received 4 months parole because she was pregnant with an unnamed man's child. Later David escaped from prison and he and Catherine started on a crime spree. This culminated in 53 counts of robbery, burglary, trespassing and driving charges. They both received short prison sentences.

Catherine lost her baby, then got her child back. She later married and had seven children and one which was killed by being run over in her driveway.

David meanwhile married after getting out of prison and was married 6 years before he suffered a head injury. Suddenly his behavior changed, and he began advertising for affairs. He later destroyed his marriage by moving his 16-year-old girlfriend into the family home.

Eventually, David decided to find Catherine. They must have been meant to be together as she promptly left her husband and her 8 children. They moved into a home as disheveled as he grew up in. Re-united with a brother in one of his later stints in prison, he then brought him home to live with them. On at least one occasion, David tried to rape his brother. On his 21st birthday, David "gifted" Catherine to him for his first-time having sex. David's sexual appetite had grown to 5 or 6 times a day and he'd developed an interest in sexual sadism.

David and Catherine eventually developed a plan for hunting young women to rape and kill. This culminated in a spree lasting about a month in 1986. They developed a code — "I have the munchies" — when they needed to communicate to each other that they liked a victim.

The team's first rape/murder was of 22-year-old Mary Nelson. She was lured to the Birnies' home and chained to the bed and David raped her while Catherine watched. Catherine took notes and pictures to learn David's preferences. After torturing and raping her multiple times, he stabbed and strangled her in a park.

Two weeks later, they picked up Susannah Candy hitchhiking. She was a 15-year-old high school straight A student. She was taken at knifepoint to the home where she was chained and raped by both the Birnies. They kept her as a sex slave a few days, then forced her to write home and call her parents, telling them she'd run away. They forced sleeping pills down her throat, then while asleep David forced Catherine to strangle Mary with an electrical cord, stating "prove you love me." She was dumped in the same park as Mary Nelson.

Next, 31-year-old former flight attendant Noelene Patterson suffered the misfortune of running out of gas. David and Catherine were recognized by Noelene since they had done work in her mother's home. They kidnapped her and for some reason Catherine felt anger and jealousy towards the elegant, accomplished, and attractive Noelene. After days of raping and abusing her, Catherine felt insecure because she could tell David seemed to like Patterson. He appeared to show reluctance in disposing of her and appeared to be putting it off. Catherine brought a knife into the room and told David to either kill "her or me." David forced sleeping pills down Noelene's throat and killed her. She was disposed of in the same park as the first 2 victims. Catherine continued her odd jealousy by throwing dirt in Noeline's face while cursing at her while they buried her.

Days later victim #4, Denise Brown, a 21-year-old computer operator was picked up at a bus stop by the couple. They took her home, repeated some of the same acts as others... forcing her to call home, forcing sleeping pills on her and raped her. She was taken to a plantation and David raped and stabbed her while Catherine held a flashlight. She was still breathing when placed in the grave, so they stabbed her with a hunting knife. Incredibly, Denise sat straight up, gasping for air in the grave. David hit her in the head with his shovel, and finally killed her with an axe. Reportedly Catherine decided she did not want to repeat this event.

Finally, their last attempted victim, Kate Moir, 17, was kidnapped while walking home. She reportedly asked, "are you going to rape me or kill me?" Kate started thinking of leaving clues for Police from the beginning. She faked eating sleeping pills and hid them. She was forced to write goodbye letters and call her parents. Then David went to work the next day, leaving Kate with Catherine. Kate was put in a bedroom while Catherine tended to a drug sale at the front door. Kate took this opportunity to leave her name in lipstick in the home and escape out a window. Police returned to the Birnies' home, finding the disgusting mess they lived in, newspaper clippings about the missing girls and other evidence. Eventually, David and Catherine confessed and took Police to the bodies.

Catherine continued her odd relationship with victim Noelene Patterson. She insisted Police go to her grave site first. She talked about Noelene and said she did not regret what they'd done to her. When they opened Noelene's grave, Catherine spit on her.

After pleading guilty to 4 murders, David Birnie hung himself by a sheet in prison in 2005. Catherine, at age 70, still looked for release from prison in 2021.

The stories of Katherine Knight, Taylor Schabusiness and Catherine Birnie, along with many other female murderers, serial killers, and team killers, provide a trove of information and psychiatric histories to provide researchers with extended study. This is without need for a constant comparison to men, nor falling back on, as one female student poignantly stated, "the broken record of Aileen Wuornos... the poster-girl for female serial murder."

REFERENCES

Dodd, Vikram. (2014, February 28). Joanna Dennehy: serial killer becomes first woman told by judge to die in jail. *The Guardian*. www.theguardian.com.

Kelleher, Michael D. & Kelleher, C.L. (1998). *Murder most rare. The female serial killer*. New York, NY. Dell/Random House.

Giannangelo, Stephen J. (2021). The Femmes Fatale. Different? They used to be. *Serial Killer Magazine*, issue 27.

Grossarth, Eric. (2021, November 12; 2022, January 6). The latest timeline in the Lori and Chad Daybell case. *EastIdahoNews.com*.

Matkin, Holly. (2022, March 2). Discovery of severed head leads to charges against woman for homicide, sexual assault. *The Police Tribune*. policetribune.com.

McIntyre, Niamh. (2017, October 27). 'Bride of Chucky' serial killer who derived sexual pleasure from killing jailed. *Independent*. www.independent.co.uk.

McNab, Duncan. (2020, December 28). Katherine Knight butchers husband, John Price, then boils his head and plates him up. *7newscom.au*.

New England Historical Society. (2021). Jolly Jane Toppan, the killer nurse obsessed with death. www.newenglandhistoricalsociety.com.

Schow, Ashe. (2022, March 2). 'Have fun trying to find all the organs': Woman kills man. Puts severed head in bucket. *The Daily Wire*. dailywire.com.

Sutton, Candace. (2019, November 26). David and Catherine Birnie: The macabre and sadistic Moorhouse murderers. *News.com.au*.

Sutton, Candace. (2021, September 2). Catherine Birnie, the 'parasite' serial killer who now wants freedom. *News.com.au.*

Vincent, Milly. (2020, June 28). Triple killer Joanna Dennehy, 37, 'is dating fellow female murderer, 25' at maximum security prison. *Daily Mail.com.* www.dailymail.uk.

Vronsky, Peter. (2007). *Female serial killers.* How and why women become monsters. New York, NY. Berkley Publishing Group.

Wade, Bethany. (2021, August 10). Inside the tale of Katherine Knight: Cannibal housewife. Film Daily. *https://filmdaily.co.*

CHAPTER 9

I Just Want To Learn from You.
Interviewing a Serial Killer.

"It's sort of along the lines as being horny. You start getting horny and it just keeps building until you have to get some relief, that is the same with the URGE to kill. It usually starts out slow and builds and you will take whatever chances necessary to satisfy it."

-David Alan Gore

Hannibal Lecter and Clarice Starling in the film "The Silence of the Lambs." (1991. Ken Regan/Orion/Kobal/Shutterstock.)

Some interviews go better than others – Hannibal and Clarice. (above)

Back in my prehistoric era, let's call it grad school, I was happily studying Clinical and

Abnormal Psychology. I reached a point where I needed to define a focus and after being riveted by the interview tapes of Kenny Bianchi of the Hillside Stranglers, I decided to tailor my studies towards serial killers and Forensic Psychology. This was harder in the early 90s, but worthwhile.

My master's thesis, a look at the then-fresh Jeffrey Dahmer case and the presentation of a psychological theory for the serial killer personality using the diathesis-stress model, sort of spiraled out of control and was eventually published as my first textbook.

Within that book, the one thing that I felt it needed was a first-hand conversation with a serial killer. I unfortunately struck out in arranging this in the time frame I had, and efforts to learn from and meet Jeffery Dahmer ended abruptly with his death in prison. Still, the point of all this is the resulting lingering need for me to interview a serial killer.

Ted Bundy speaks to Dr. James Dobson.
(1989, Bradford County, USA. Mark Foley/AP/Shutterstock.)

There's been plenty of interviews with serial murderers published and videorecorded. Some good, some not. A famous example of one is the interview conducted by Dr. James Dobson with Ted Bundy, hours before his execution in 1989. This interview has received its share of criticism, mainly for the apparent use of the interview to further Dr. Dobson's crusade against pornography. I find such criticisms to be unnecessarily dismissive. I don't have a problem with Dobson using this vehicle to promote his own agenda while sitting down with a Ted Bundy. The fact is this conversation was fascinating, and I've seen it used in a number of teaching venues, from psychology to criminology to law enforcement classes on interview and interrogation. Whether Bundy is lying, being manipulative, insincere, psychopathic, isn't the point. Listening to what he said and how he said it hours before his execution was a learning opportunity that we should thank Dobson for. I still use the film, *Fatal Addiction*, in my classes.

And regarding pornography, my own interview with a killer in 2012 brought up this topic, one I'd personally dismissed, and forced me to reconsider previously held positions, providing yet another example of the necessity to continue learning about the overall subject of serial murder and refining my knowledge base as time passes.

Another example is the book, *The Last Victim* (1999) by Jason Moss. Briefly, Moss seems to wear the shell of different personalities in order to appeal to different killers in order to meet and speak with them, most notably John Wayne Gacy. In one passage Moss described his intent and technique with Gacy:

> At this point I knew I had Gacy's attention, but the question was, for how long? I had no idea how many others were competing for his time and attention. To ensure that I remained his focus, I decided in my next letter, to continue modelling myself on his "ideal victim" by painting myself as both sexually active and submissive.

> Even though I knew Gacy was playing with me, I was nevertheless flattered. Just as I'd selected him out of hundreds of Death Row predators to write to, he'd selected me to focus on out of hundreds of academics, voyeurs, and would-be disciples vying for his attention.

> I'd earned the devil's nod.

This work has been criticized as manipulative and dangerous among other comments, but again, I think if someone takes it at its face and learns what they can, it's another experience that people should benefit from as it's a rare occurrence to have these meetings and conversations.

In my book, *Real-Life Monsters: A Psychological Examination of the Serial Murderer*, I recounted the events surrounding my correspondence and later interviews with a serial killer. In the Chapter entitled, *"An Interview with a Monster?"* I went through the phases of searching for an appropriate subject for this endeavor. I'll admit this is my favorite chapter in that book, one that involved a visceral, physical experience on multiple occasions and produced and experience that I can't compare to any other.

Reviewer Dr. Katherine Ramsland, writing about the book for *Psychology Today* in her blog Shadow Boxing, referred to the chapter as "riveting." This is the highest compliment to me coming from Dr. Ramsland, as that chapter felt like it was an effort that deserved a book of its own.

I don't want to re-print that chapter here, but I'll provide some background. I'd written my first text, *The Psychopathology of Serial Murder: A Theory of Violence* in 1996. I was quite pleased with this effort, but as I set out to write again about the topic after 16 years of criminology and psychology study, the first thing I needed to add was a serial killer interview. I'd run into roadblocks in efforts to speak to Jeffrey Dahmer and Henry Lee Lucas back in the day and finding an interview subject for a new work was an even greater challenge.

I corresponded with several killers, some well-known, some not known at all. I wasn't convinced that a well-known offender was necessarily the preferred choice beyond a certain acceptance by some readers and possibly as a sales enhancer. However, my feeling was the quality and depth of the conversation was more important than the fame or the graphic nature of the kills.

In preparation, I tried to research the best way to accomplish this. My supervisor at the time was a former prison warden and I asked him for ideas. He put me in touch with a prison representative who offered me some key points. She said I needed to create my own relationship with a subject, rather than see how a prison could help. I'd need to develop that personal situation, be added to that person's visitors list, and go from there. Each state and facility would have their own rules and requirements and I'd need to research that.

I tried many sources. Rodney Alcala told me he didn't want to talk about it and referred me to an attorney to buy his book. Keith Jesperson didn't seem like a good candidate. Leslie Van Houten and several others wouldn't respond. Gwendolyn Graham wanted me to prove her innocence.

I landed on the offender I would eventually write about after a suggestion by a friend who'd had a lot of experience in killer correspondence and said this person would politely write back to most respectful first letters. He resisted my overtures to interview him in-depth repeatedly, telling me he wasn't proud, but embarrassed by his history. He suggested people who would be eager to speak to me from Death Row, some who had killed in entertainingly graphic manners. A machete came up in one conversation. In the end, I stuck with this guy, and it was the right choice.

A controversial decision I made was that I agreed not to reveal the killer's name. This was key in getting him to agree to in-depth discussion, as he was always concerned about blow-back on his family as well as his own security in the prison. Once we settled on this, the conversations took on a much more open feel, I think. I had concerns about credibility, and possibly less interest in the book without a loud killer's name to attach to it. In retrospect, I think it was a good decision. If Oprah wants to play Gotcha with me, I'll appear on her show with a ton of proof as to my conversations. I've had students over the years love this aspect of the chapter, and some hate it. Side note: As I was writing this chapter, I had one student come to me after class with a list of "finalists" he'd selected as possibly the killer I'd interviewed. The correct name was not included. However, another student completed the Final Exam, and added a note to it saying he'd "cracked the case and the killer was…" And he was right.

The offender is a serial killer that those who have studied the topic might have heard of. He's easily found in the research. He was convicted of Armed Violence, Aggravated Kidnapping, Aggravated Criminal Sexual Assault, Escape from a Penal Institution, Aggravated Battery, and multiple counts of Murder. Of course, I needed to research his crimes, the newspaper accounts, and his history in prison, which included the interesting escape charge.

It made sense to me to get a feel for who he was. I bought some letters of his from a murderabilia website. It was clear he spoke to the ladies a bit differently than to me (shocking) but he was consistently polite, reserved, seemingly earnest in the topic discussion and no more phony than some people I might go to lunch with this week.

It was interesting how defensive he was about murderabilia sales and being exploited. I certainly didn't ask him for anything, didn't suggest he paint bloody skulls for me with victims' names on them. I have an extensive file of hand-written letters from our entire correspondence in binders, but I highly doubt these would be as important to anyone as they are to me. I certainly wouldn't consider selling them.

As I was warned, I needed to understand that prison's security requirements. He was transferred a couple times during our talks, but they were within the same state and procedures did not really vary. The most difficult thing I found was that I was not allowed any sort of equipment for recording… no phone, no video, no cameras for photos, no tape recorders, no pens, paper, or pencils. Nothing. It did not affect me logistically like I thought… when we ended our hours-long conversations, I'd sit in the prison parking lot and dump everything on paper, and it was loud and clear what he said. This affected me a bit when conducting the interviews as I had no script or outline, but I did have one in the car and made myself very familiar with the conversation route I wanted to take. I did follow up by letter on points or clarifications or particular questions I did not remember when in the interview, and many quotes I used from him were word-for-word taken from letters in his handwriting.

More prison logistics: I had to be included on his visitors list and I would tell him ahead of time a couple potential dates I might be there, so he would expect me. Sometimes I couldn't get in for some reason. Sometimes there were lockdowns and they told me to go home. I did not have any problems with Corrections personnel at all. At first, I felt like they looked at me funny, but later visits were quicker in the security measures and procedure. Some Corrections Officers just passed on the extent of inspection they used to perform when I first started visiting.

I did send him my first book early in our talks so he would have some reference to who I was and that I was not making up the educational aspect of this project. He clearly did not like media and even called John Douglas "a psychopath." He never did receive it. Many months later he found out that it was intercepted by prison officials who felt it was a topic that could be considered "inflammatory" for a violent sexually sadistic inmate. The least they could have done was mail it back, though.

From a personal relationship aspect, I wanted to establish trust and rapport like any other interviewer. I did not want to appear to be a groupie or a weirdo or someone not to be taken seriously. It was critical to me that I establish mutual respect, not hero worship, not best buds, but respect between 2 people trying to accomplish something together. Of course, I had to be cognizant of being "played" by a psychopath, at the very least a manipulative person who would benefit by using me as a person who could color his story. However, this is where the anonymity of his identity played in my favor. There's no real upside for him to lie to me, Is there? Maybe there was.

Honestly, there was a minimum of bullshit by either of us. He called me on being too agreeable at times and I never flinched from hard questions he had, like when he asked me if I thought he was a psychopath. I did not feel like there were excuses being thrown around by him. He did blame the victims a bit when he said the women needed to be more aware of their surroundings and better protect themselves from people like him, but frankly, I give that advice to any woman that will listen to me, student or not.

I've had plenty of offender and witness conversations in my career, both interviews and interrogations. This was clearly to be an interview, not an interrogation, and I did not want to corner him or move him into any particular direction. I wanted him to be truthful. I wanted to open doors for him to think about, maybe for the first time, and possibly discover something. I believe my strongest objective was to get him to understand that all I wanted to do was to learn from him… who he was, how he got where he is. Luckily, he felt the same way and wanted to get there, too. We did not come up with some epiphany that a therapist might have accomplished, but we had open, frank talks that were interesting and insightful. I do truly believe he benefitted from our conversations. Any researcher or interviewer should consider that a worthy goal.

I needed to be mindful of my book's impending deadline, so I pushed for in-person conversations when I concluded he was the right subject. I did keep in mind techniques like the Reid Interview method, thinking about Behavior Symptom Analysis which include observations of physical behavior, verbal, and nonverbal behavior. I routinely utilized open questions, direct questions, and immediate follow-ups for clarification. It was important to me to lay out a direction, get him talking and then shut up and let him talk, which is a habit I got into in my criminal investigations over the years.

My personal reaction was that he tried to appear as human as possible. I felt like the few times we touched on remorse, that it was not there. There were major consistencies with the Ted Bundy/Dr. Dobson interviews that come to mind. I believed the majority of what he told me. The most disappointing aspect was there was no smoking gun that resulted, no blinking sign that pointed to an obvious origin. If anything, my interviews with this person highlighted the incredible difficulty there is when trying to dissect a serial murderer's development. He told me from the outset that doctors and researchers "paint with too broad a brush," and I think this was the most important thing he taught me. These killers do have a certain amount of consistency sometimes, and some of them have horrific stories of abuse, mistreatment, and attachment difficulties. But some are simply not that easy to peel back.

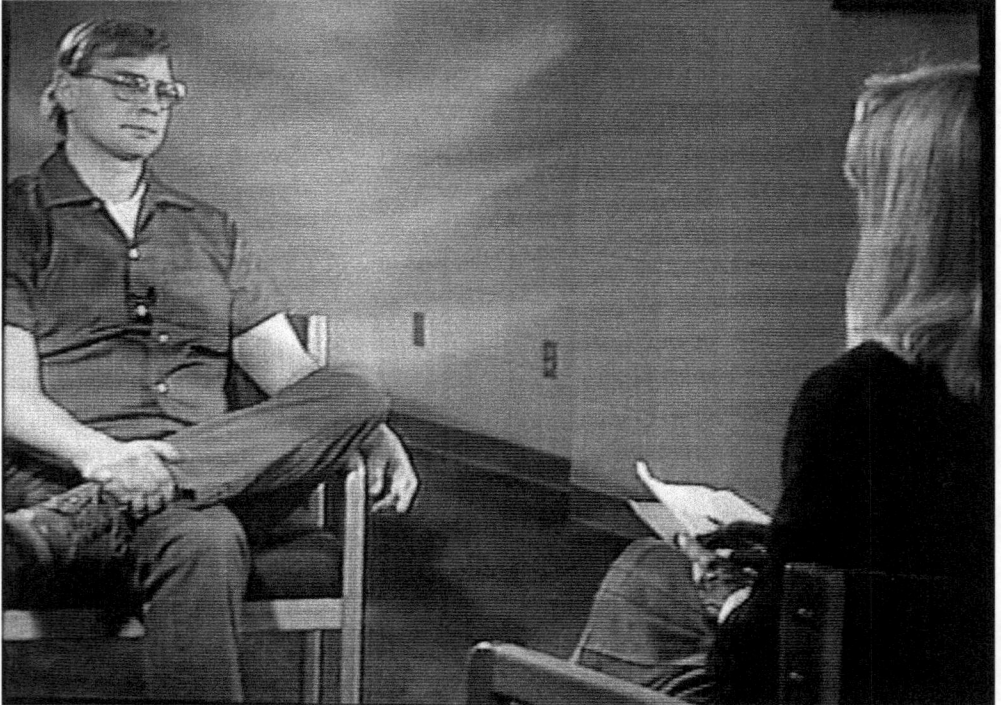

Inside Edition/Jeffrey Dahmer.
(1993. Milwaukee, USA. Anonymous/AP/Shutterstock.)

I'm confident that he did get something from our time together. I felt the most anxiety when, as promised, I sent him a copy of the completed chapter about him for feedback. His biggest complaint was the title: *An Interview with a Monster?* "Was that really necessary, Steve? A monster?" I logically said it was consistent with the book title, and we let that topic go. He did comment that I'd treated him fairly, accurately represented what he said and felt, and lived up to my promises of respect and treating him professionally. That was a good day.

In my class I have the students review the textbook for reactions and feedback. Once they get past the need to pander and suck up to the professor, they do offer some terrific insights and observations, things I keep notes of. Everyone loves to guess who the killer is; few get it right. The students love the interview aspects and want more of them. I agree they are a highlight to a text on Serial Murder, but they must be conducted properly. The best comment, I think, is when they say, "it felt real."

PERSONAL VISITS

There's a lot of ways to consider the idea of interviewing a serial killer. Some individuals simply want to visit these people due to their own interest in the subject, from a psychological, personal, historical and curiosity level. I suppose it's semantics to decide whether this is "interviewing" as opposed to corresponding or visiting an incarcerated person. I think any level of correspondence, visitation, interview, or even interrogations will have its nuances and overlap.

One person I met who has engaged in this activity at length is a woman named Ashleigh Keto. Ashleigh is a 33-year-old woman originally from New Orleans who has visited several offenders over the years and established many personal relationships. Some of her experiences provide a lot of insight. The following is the Q & A exchange she graciously agreed to share:

Ashleigh, please answer whatever questions you feel like or are comfortable in answering. Don't hesitate to skip what you would prefer not to talk about. Please confirm this is your correct name spelling. Is it OK that I quote you and use your name? Do you have any concerns about this? Can I use your age?

Ashleigh Keto is correct. I am thirty-three years of age and I do not mind if you quote me.

Do you have a personal/professional background that's related to this activity? Are they involved in studies?

I do have a degree in criminal justice, and psychology. I at one point... had a great interest to study and research the psychological aspects of serial murders which led me to getting my second degree I mentioned, but I have never utilized it or furthered down that path... so definitely not involved in my current affairs. I wish it were... who knows what the future holds.

Tell me about your beginnings. How did you get involved in visiting serial killers? How long have you done this? Have you visited other types of offenders?

I first wrote to Peter Sutcliffe when I was 17 years old. Peter was overseas and it took about a month to get a response. I don't have a memory of "what" got me into serial killers so to speak, but I have always been drawn to the macabre as long as I can remember. The macabre and outcast things are where I tend to shine and once I made a connection with Mr. Sutcliffe it was like I found my niche! So I branched out! I have been doing this just shy of 17 years. I made friends with someone I consider a fabulous person in California named William & he is the one who finally talked me into branching out from phone calls & letters to visiting death row inmates. I generally would only visit condemned inmates, but I had a pen pal who I found off a pen pal site once that was incarcerated for 5 years for vehicular homicide for being intoxicated and his passenger did not have a seat-belt on and well... did not end so well for her. Very sad and I was more than happy to offer my friendship. He is now a free man and we are still Facebook friends. I have wrote to and befriended all sorts such as Jeremy Christian, and I have wrote a couple offenders for a short period who were on the registry in California for unspeakable crimes.

What has been your main interest in visiting? Did you want to accomplish something in particular?

To see what that side of life is like and how being mentally ill really destroys lives. I also just like to hear people's stories whether it is the reality of compartmentalizing separate lives being lived simultaneously. I also have a great interest in how the system works and does not work. I am interested... in it all. All the way down to much humanity goes into the system or lack thereof in some cases. Now that is just me being a sap because I know it is not to be a retreat.

How do you choose inmates to visit?

I generally go for inmates who have murdered ten plus victims in a very brutal manner or went undetected for a while. Very interested by the atrocities and seeing the other side of those individuals.

Have you ever felt personally unsafe or otherwise concerned?

Not really. I mean I was nervous at my first San Quentin death row visit because they lock you in a cage with them for 5 hours if you are traveling far. I was coming from New Orleans, so I got the extended visit. I stood 5' 3" and 135 pounds soaking wet and the inmate I was visiting was 6' 3" 6'4"? 300 pounds of muscle, so he towered over me and I just remember being told that one officer is not coming in for you alone if something goes wrong. That concerned me! Then I remembered he was my "friend" so to speak and serial killers do not usually kill their friends and that is how I made it through that visit (that is my story and I am sticking to it!)

Tell me about some of the recognizable names you have encountered.

I have been on several visiting lists! Roy Norris, Dennis BTK Rader (very close friend), Bobby Joe Long, Phillip Jablonski, Elmer Wayne Henley, Robin Gecht.

I have also had the pleasure of conversing with Robert Bardo, Chester Turner, Robert Yates, Keith Jesperson (no interest on my end to continue correspondence), Jodi Arias, I have also met Scott Peterson at San Quentin!

Some of them, like Elmer Wayne Henley are your friends. Is that usually the case?

Not always, but sometimes you find a diamond in the dust. For me Wayne is that diamond and Dennis is right there a close second. Wayne has been the greatest friend! He is a smart man and his mother even sends me baked goods and Christmas presents every year! His little brother also sends me things also. We are like family to be honest he has seen me through some very dark periods in my life and I would not trade him for all the outside friends in the world.

Do they shy away from talking about their cases?

Most of them do... I do not make it a point to even ask about the crimes. I feel like that is just rude and besides you can only have so many conversations about people's crimes. It is just not feasible to occupy years of friendship by talking about their crimes over and over. I did have one pen pal in the past that loved to speak about his crimes though and that was Phillip Jablonski. I asked him once if he were ever freed from prison again would he stay out or kill again? He did not hesitate at all to respond with "I would go back, I like to kill people." I also remember inquiring if he murdered his wife and her mother because they made him angry. He replied, "No, I just knew it would be a while before anyone realized they were missing." YIKES! Now that is an evil person, but he had his moments of being fun to speak to. He kept up on current events etc. I have only slightly touched on a certain crime that happened on January 15th, 1974, but not in great detail and I do not wanna go into that in detail while my "friend" is still alive.

Tell me about some of the more memorable conversations and relationships.

I truly miss my friend Bobby Joe Long. I was devastated when he was executed. I remember writing the governor and feeling so helpless to be able to do anything in regards to his life. I never got to speak to him on the phone. Florida inmates only receive one fifteen-minute phone call a month, so he would use it to call his mother which I thought was nice. He really had a great personality and built such a strong sense of self through pen on paper. I wept watching his execution. I have not obtained any new death row inmates outside of California due to the fact I never want to experience that loss again. It sounds silly, but we all have something to offer one another albeit some minuscule.

Do any simply just try to scare you? Do you feel like you are lied to often?

I have not experienced this, and any lies I ever heard were corny ones attempting to sound cool or "puffing their chest out"

I've encountered concerns from inmates regarding their safety in prison related to interviews. Has this come up?

Everyone that I pen to are housed in Segregation or Safety housing blocks, so I have not heard too much of this with the people I know. I would imagine Gen Pop probably is pretty scary.

I've also encountered concerns about being used for memorabilia and/or being exploited. Have you? Have any been concerned about what you might share with another inmate?

Martin Kipp was concerned that I was writing other people in San Quentin when I was writing to him. Apparently that is like a no-no in this community that you should make sure your pen friends are not incarcerated in the same facility. I do not think it should hold any count if it is platonic!

Tell me what you think is the most different about your personal visits as compared to someone going in doing research or study. Could one "agenda" benefit by thinking about the other?

I think the inmates can tell when someone is being a "real person" they tend to open up to you more… share more intimate things with you… let's face it… someone doing an interview from Fox News is not going to talk about their personal life, so to get someone to open up that reciprocity helps. I absolutely believe there is some benefit to be had from the other, but I also believe inmates would see through to the other side if you catch my drift.

Tell me anything of interest or relevance that I might have missed. Is there something you would like to share or point out as important?

Not off the top of my head, but I happy to answer any questions in the future or give a female perspective on the topic in the future.

I believe interviews and exchanges with offenders are of enormous value. I believe every one conducted can be dissected and analyzed and researchers can learn from both the good and the bad of these efforts. In other chapters in this book, I mention an unsuccessful attempt at speaking with Ted Kaczynski and a very successful exchange I had with a woman who committed a multiple murder. Those insights, I believe, are priceless and are worth pursuing.

REFERENCES

Fatal Addiction. (1989). Final Interview with Ted Bundy with James Dobson. (video) Focus on the Family.

Giannangelo, Stephen J. (2012). *Real Life Monsters: A psychological examination of the serial murderer*. Santa Barbara, CA. ABC-CLIO.

Moss, Jason. (1999). *The last victim. A true-life journey into the mind of the serial killer*. New York, NY. Grand Central Publishing.

Ramsland, Katherine. (2012) Shadow boxing: Homicidal pattern disorder. *Psychology Today*.

CHAPTER 10

Conversations.
An Atypical Offender, an Exorcist and Mental Illness.

"I just felt like I had no mind. I just felt something else was controlling, controlling me."

-David Berkowitz

(Photographee.eu/Shutterstock.)

Some conversations are just unlike any others.

In this chapter, I had the opportunity to exchange ideas and thoughts with a couple of fascinating individuals, people whose personal experiences and challenges provide information that's hard to extract from a text.

The two subjects of this chapter have been on very different points in their exposure to severe mental illness. Their stories follow.

PSYCHOSIS AND MURDER... FROM THE INSIDE

This story isn't about a monster. Or a serial killer. Or even a mass murder according to criminologists' definitions. A woman shot her husband and another relative in a tragic, horrible mental illness nightmare. This is about what it meant to reflect on the horror from the offender's point of view. It's a discussion not often presented within criminal psychology study.

THE CRIMES

The newspaper coverage wasn't anything that would garner the attention of the networks looking for a juicy story. A woman was charged with first-degree murder in the shooting deaths of her husband and another relative which occurred in their home. Both men were shot multiple times. In her first appearance in court, she was wearing an anti-suicide smock with her hands cuffed in front of her. The woman entered a not guilty plea and bond was set at 10 million dollars.

Police said earlier that the shootings at the home apparently resulted from a domestic disturbance. Records showed the husband had filed for divorce due to irreconcilable differences. The woman faced life in prison.

Both men were fondly remembered by friends and family. One was described as a nice man, who "had nothing bad to say about anybody." The other as always having a smile on his face and loving to laugh... "one of the nicest guys I ever met."

Three years later, accounts show the woman was sentenced to 40 years in prison after pleading guilty but mentally ill to first and second-degree murder. The sentences were to be served consecutively, meaning she would not be released until her 80s.

A psychiatric report showed some evidence that she was suffering from "major depressive disorder with possible psychotic features" at the time of the murders. She was found fit to stand trial, and that her condition did not mean she was legally insane.

A second-degree murder charge was added, indicating that she acted under "the sudden and intense heat of passion" and unreasonably believed her actions were justifiable.

Emotional comments by victims' family members followed, as would be expected. "Our family has been destroyed by an act of evil and hatred," said one relative. She hoped the defendant would find remorse and that "time will heal my family's broken heart." A prosecutor remarked that, "the defendant was found accountable for her actions."

THE PERSONAL SIDE

I know this woman as a friend. Known her for decades. She's a fun loving, quirky, highly intelligent, interesting person. I have no possible way of knowing what went on in her home or personal life and have no intention to make excuses or justifications for what happened. I'm not qualified to do that, and I'm certainly not informed enough. It would be inappropriate and unfair to everyone involved.

However, I read the facts of this case and the fact that this woman made no attempt to place the blame anywhere but on herself is notable. I see that she pleaded Guilty but Mentally Ill (GBMI) and did not attempt a different diminished capacity defense that would allow her to walk.

I believe another person may have attempted a different defense, one that did not come with agreeing to most likely spending the rest of her natural life in prison. As far as I know, there's no evidence of her trying to shift blame or escaping responsibility or lack of remorse.

This is one reason I wanted to hear her perspective on this event, a perspective rarely heard by anyone. Even though I've studied mental illness at length through graduate school, I have to admit looking at it on the pages of a textbook is different than attempting to walk in those shoes.

I recall a personal experience with someone who was close to me years ago, who was suffering with bipolar disorder. This individual chose not to take medication (other than the self-administered kind) and attempted to ride it out alone. The eventual effect on their personal life was substantial, and the real-life consequences, significant. But the thing that stands out the most to me that while the parameters of the disease were recognizable from a scholastic standpoint, the actual descriptions and layers of these experiences as described to me by a person in those shoes were something at quite another level.

That case and the one I'm about to describe are examples of studying particular pathologies at length, but when exposed to the real-life details of the human experience, understanding it from a different perspective.

OUR CONVERSATIONS

The following is a summary of our correspondence. It's choppy, random, and barely sequential in timing. These are the thoughts she was able to convey to me, someone whose studied mental illness, but never experienced what she was about to describe.

I received a response to my first letter quite some time after I sent it. I just wanted to talk a bit about what she had experienced. It was short and written on the back of a page from a coloring book. She said she wasn't interested in discussing the case with anyone. I understood.

We spoke again, mostly catching up, talking about our sports teams.

A subsequent letter included correspondence she'd written and put aside and lost, written before the first response I'd received. It was more insightful, explaining that she didn't know how she felt about talking about it all, that it was hard to articulate. She didn't know if she wanted to dredge up old emotions. She wasn't sure how much she remembers. She did say that right after it happened, it sounded like it happened to someone else, and she was simply told about it. It didn't seem real.

She explained that she had a psychotic break. Part of the experience was that she knew something was wrong, but she wouldn't know how to put it into words, what to say at a hospital, how to explain what she was experiencing to a doctor. The ability to articulate to another person did not seem like a viable option.

When the shootings occurred, her mom, her main source of support, was not home, and things just didn't work out. She knew she needed help but didn't know what kind of help she needed.

She also mentioned a challenge with cancer.

By our next conversation, she was more comfortable in the discussion and was more able to collect her thoughts. She drew a laugh from me as she actually remembered my returned mail from Jeffrey Dahmer in 1994 (pictured in Chapter 2). I don't know two other people who remember that happening.

But she went on to describe her experiences. Some people had noticed a change in her behavior, but she held it all in and was a private person and didn't discuss it with anyone.

She described her personal situation as not a sudden development, that it was a gradually building stress and paranoia. But when she <u>knew</u> (her emphasis) she wasn't OK (she had been handling the stress OK before this) it happened immediately. She then made a wrong decision, failing to go to a hospital or speak to someone close to her.

We discussed the concept of dissociation when she talked about "feeling like it all happened to someone else." She agreed that my explanation of dissociation described it perfectly.

She described a feeling of no input in what was about to happen. "I felt like a robot with pre-programmed instructions," she said, "with no sense of questioning."

At the full psychotic break, she knew something was terribly wrong, but didn't know how to describe it. Just knew she needed help. Again, she described an inability to articulate what was going on in her head, and no way to access the help and support she desperately needed.

At this point all apparent options failed. (No close friend available, mom was not nearby, and a dead phone) She still didn't know what to tell a hospital. It seemed like every detail had conspired against her.

It was all less than a dream in her view, because sometimes dreams felt real. It wasn't described as a dreamlike state, or comparable to a dream, but as something that couldn't be considered real.

The next day she said it felt like an event "someone told me about 30 years ago." Her memory was foggy and stated she would have believed anything she was told at that point.

She said in court she was found GBMI, pointing out this is why her sentence is "so much lighter than it could have been." This light sentence was for 40 years. The newspaper reported she got 20 years for the GBMI count and 20 for the 2nd Degree Murder count.

She later described her overall state of mind:

> In the middle of my turmoil, before anything had happened I could not get my thoughts together – not even for a single thought. I was very, very confused. My mind flashed an image and I saw a large pot of water with letters of the alphabet all mixed up in this pot of water like a big alphabet soup. I wanted all those letters to come together to help me form a thought, but they just wouldn't. It's hard to describe how disjointed thoughts are. It's NOT like it's part of one thought followed by part of another thought, it's more like maybe what dementia might feel like. I do remember asking myself, "is this what insanity feels like?" as I stared at the alphabet soup. And was unable to put the letters together to form a thought. But I 'reasoned' that if I was really insane I wouldn't know to question whether I was insane so I (wrongly, apparently) assumed I was not insane.

> Once I was removed from the situation and felt safe (and knew my mom was safe) and I was able to sleep a lot of the issues resolved. Of course, with the crime new issues emerged. It's been a slow process and my grief will never be over. I'll take that to my grave. When I think about it, I wish I'd never been born or wish I had taken my own life which is what my first thought was when I got home. It would have been better in the long run on everyone if I had just done that, though I have helped many people (inmates, charities, ministries, etc.) since then.

Regarding the insanity defense and mental illness:

> There is no "temporary insanity" defense. I WAS found guilty of "Guilty, But Mentally Ill" (GBMI) which is not the same as "Not Guilty by Reason of Insanity." (NGBRI). Being found GBMI sends you to prison but may reduce the amount of time you spend in prison. Another option to GBMI and NGBRI is to be put in a mental institution until you're fit to stand trial. Then you go to trial and are found GBMI or NGBRI.

> There are people here who are so insane but found only mentally ill that

they will swallow light bulbs, batteries and everything else they can get their hands on. Another inmate punctures herself with a pen or whatever else is available and then rubs her own feces in the wound. Another inmate plucked both of her eyeballs out of their sockets and onto the floor without even crying out in pain.

She does look back and think about being insane and questioning whether she was insane and deciding she was not and now looking back and feeling she clearly was. She likened it to dreaming and in the middle of it wondering if you are dreaming, deciding you are not and then waking up later to realize you really were in a dream.

This woman does in fact still struggle with the wish that she had taken her own life, but I will say she has taken some satisfaction in some of these conversations. I did tell her that I'd used these personal raw insights in my classes and in teaching people about the realities of mental illness, and this meant a great deal to her. She does seek to find ways to affect people around her in a positive manner as often as possible, while she faces down the emotional and physical challenges that likely will remain in her path for the rest of her days.

EXPERIENCES WITH MENTALLY ILL INMATES

Most recent correspondence has included a couple interesting stories about mentally ill inmates my friend shares her space with sometimes.

One woman, incarcerated for murder, reportedly has multiple personalities, 3 separate personalities from her "host," I'm told. She explains:

> She experiences auditory hallucinations and is constantly in communication with her other voices. These include a "little girl" voice that she talks in, an "adult lady" and a "man." When these voices come out (which is near constantly) her voice takes on the tone of that personality and often the voices will tell her what she can or cannot do. All the voices are out loud.

So, by her description these conflicts and interactions play out in public, all voiced by the inmate:

> If the voices tell her not to take a particular medicine (for some reason she has an intense aversion to TUMS) she will throw the pill across the floor.

And, if the nurse says she must take it, her "normal" self will argue out loud with the voice telling her not to take it. She will say "it's not my fault, she's making me take it," the "she" is the nurse. The argument will go back and forth and if the nurse is persistent enough the inmate will take the pill eventually.

The woman's behavior was described as suddenly throwing things like cups, hair ties or whatever she can get her hands on, as directed by the voices. This woman was a roommate for about a week. At one point, she was going to show some pictures but suddenly put them away. She explained she was told by her voices that she wasn't allowed to show them.

Later on:

I was pouring hot water into the inmate's cup so she could have coffee when she started arguing with the voices… I heard her say "you can't throw that on her!" I moved away from her before anything happened.

Reportedly the inmate could be focused on a conversation or playing cards where the voices would diminish, but any lull in the conversation and the voices would start immediately.

She's described as "lucid and sweet" when she "is herself," but would always clearly need a care-giver regardless of her residency status.

Another inmate she described that was alluded to earlier:

Another sad case is an inmate who killed her baby. She kept "seeing his face" so she quietly (they say she didn't make a sound) plucked both of her eyeballs out and onto the floor. She believed that would stop the visions of her dead baby. For a long time (and maybe still) she thought the doctor here could put her eyeballs back in so she could see again. Of course, that is not possible, so now she lives here and is blind.

Both of these women are described as more docile than the rest of the women in population.

USING THIS PRICELESS INFORMATION

The fact is this information and insight is simply not available anywhere under any other circumstances than from the mental health sufferer's own mouth, heart, and mind. It's another example of the most valuable information and educational opportunity come from real people in real experiences. I cannot imagine the pain and difficulty involved in re-living and articulating these experiences and emotions.

However, I am confident that there's a slice of positivity that comes with sharing this information that continues to be directly shared with students of all types. Helping them to learn the impact and the connection of mental illness to some of the most extreme behaviors is the ultimate goal of education, and I'm glad it can continue to give her a sense of purpose.

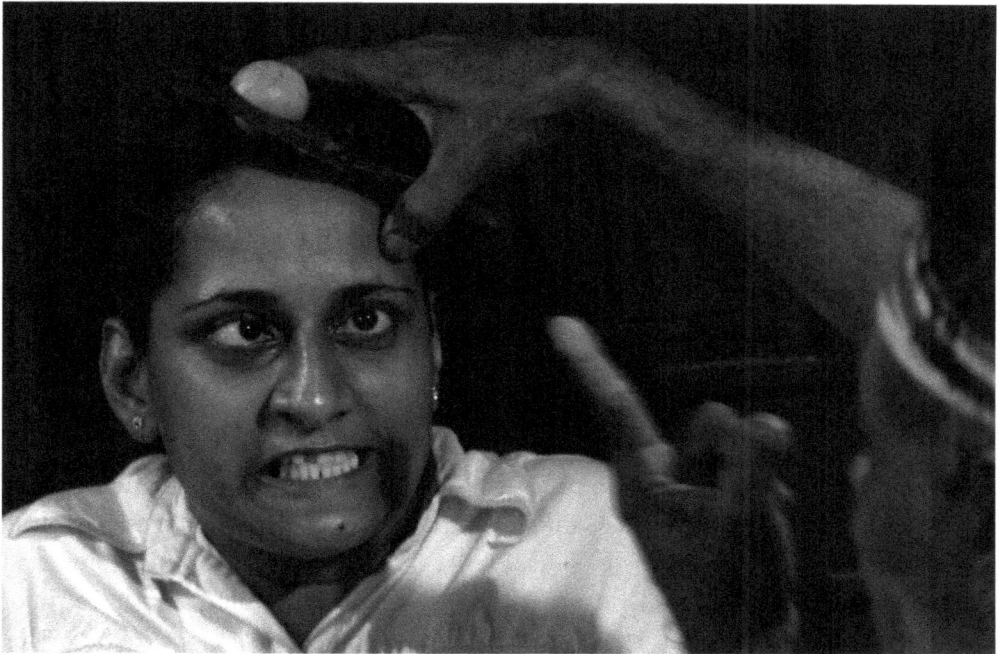

An exorcist holds a lime on a struggling afflicted female.
(Sri Lanka Thovil- Feb 2012. M A Pushpa Kumara/ERA/Shutterstock.)

A CONVERSATION WITH AN EXORCIST

While I'm recounting fascinating, real-life conversations with those who can offer a unique perspective on homicide, mental illness and beyond, I must present the conversation I had with an actual exorcist.

Murderers have long been associated with orders from God or demonic possession. Deanna Laney, of Tyler, Texas said God spoke to her, ordering her to kill her sons to prove her faith. Laney did so, smashing their heads with large rocks. She was acquitted by reason of insanity and was released from an institution in 2012 after only 8 years. Andrea Yates, in a highly publicized case, drowned her 5 children after believing she was possessed by Satan himself. She later said she saw and spoke to Satan in her cell. She felt the possession was so complete she could only destroy him by her own execution. She felt the presence of Satan within her, stated Dr. Phillip Resnick. He asked her to clarify if she meant she was possessed by a demon. "No," she said, "the one and only Satan was literally within me."

Exorcism is a topic that's enthralled many, probably most through Hollywood depictions such as William Peter Blatty's 1973 film, *The Exorcist* and subsequent sequels and other lesser-known films on the large and small screen.

Exorcism is the religious or spiritual act of expelling demons or other spiritual entities from a person who is believed to be possessed. Once rare in the United States, it's increased due to media attention. Though westerners usually associate exorcism with Christianity, it can be found in other religions too. Exorcism can be found in the religions of Hinduism, Buddhism, Taoism, Islam, and Judaism. Various rituals and processes are practiced, depending on the culture and religion. Countries with an increased activity include Mexico, Brazil, and The United Kingdom, but exorcism is increasingly widespread around the world.

The Roman Catholic Archdiocese of Washington defines exorcism as, "The Rite of Exorcism is a sacramental of the Catholic Church whereby the Church asks publicly and authoritatively in the name of Jesus Christ that a person or object be protected against the power of the Evil One and withdrawn from his dominion" (Catechism of the Catholic Church #1673). It is "directed at the expulsion of demons or to the liberation from demonic possession through the spiritual authority which Jesus entrusted to His Church."

According to the United States Conference of Catholic Bishops, there are 2 types of exorcisms. "Exorcisms are divided into two kinds (or forms)." Simple or minor forms of exorcism are found in two places: first, for those preparing for Baptism, the *Rite of Christian Initiation of Adults* (RCIA) and the *Rite of Baptism for Children* both call for minor exorcisms; secondly, the appendix of *Exorcisms and Related Supplications* includes a series of prayers which may be used by the faithful.

The second kind is the solemn or "major exorcism," which is a rite that can only be performed by a bishop or a by priest, with the special and express permission of the local ordinary (cf. Code of Canon Law, can. 1172). This form is directed "at the expulsion of demons or to the liberation [of a person] from demonic possession" (*Catechism of the Catholic Church*, no. 1673).

However, those of us interested in clinical and abnormal psychology and their history have always looked at the topic of possession and resulting exorcisms as likely a confluence of the existence of severe mental illness, significant organic disorders such as brain tumors, or a combination of both.

And, while one must consider the possibility of an actual demon possession to be among the unlikeliest of events, anyone who has even a passing belief in Christianity must at least consider the possibility of demon possession or influence from Satan, Lucifer, or Beelzebub himself.

In my travels, I met a Catholic Priest who has had some experience with the topic of exorcism. We instantly shared a common interest in human abnormal psychology and the periphery, including how mental illness might intersect with the concept of exorcism. I asked him to answer a few of my questions on the subject, which opened a door, I think, which could lead to chapters unto themselves. Still, it's an interesting opening exchange into a subject I feel many should find fascinating. These questions and answers follow.

Father Casey told me he solicited input from his presiding bishop on his answers, which I appreciated.

Father, could you please provide your full name and title? Do you mind if I quote you and use your real name?

Father Casey Scruggs, Priest.

Please tell me a little about your background and how you came to have the experiences you have had.

My personal history begins in Tennessee, born into a missionary Baptist family. The church was built with logs from the family farm in the 1860s, and that church is still going today. This basic upbringing in faith, began my understanding in the world. The Calvinist nature of the sermons, while helpful, left me wanting to understand more, as they seemed to pick and choose from scripture, leaving out some pretty relevant verses, in favor of the (get saved before you die as the main course of the meal). I then went to many different denominations of churches, to see the differing views. At 17, joining the military, with deployments to the Middle East and Central America, where my spiritual path was not lost to me, meeting and learning from those people I came in contact with, as if on the path. That phrase can be the sum of the question, on the path. I have met a leader from the Ashanti tribe from Africa, lived and did ceremony with the Lakota on the Rosebud reservation, to include the vision quest and their sacred Sundance. The list goes on, my point being, all roads lead to somewhere. In my case, all these experiences and blessed meetings led to the path I am on. Each teaching lessons about their spiritual culture, life, God, history, people. This varied opening to understanding, help to form my path forward in negotiating the spiritual side of life and intervening for those in need. There are requirements listed in the Roman Ritual. A priest expressly and in special wise authorized by the Ordinary, must be properly distinguished for his piety, prudence, and integrity of life. Should fulfil his duty undertaking in all constancy and humility, being immune to striving for human aggrandizement and relying not upon his own but upon the power of God. Should be of mature years (50 or around, I am 50 now) and revered not alone for his office but his moral qualities. Another answer for this and the question regarding experience with exorcism is also listed in the Roman Ritual requirements: In order to exercise his ministry rightly, he should resort to a great deal more study of the matter.

Some killers, most notably Richard Ramirez, have openly embraced the concept of Satanism. How do you feel an offender's history plays into this?

Great question. People in the world have always tried to conquer or manipulate the forces and circumstances around them. From animists who see spirits in everything around them that are controlling everything to the cultures who use their forebears for information on the future or attacks on other tribes or individuals. Still today, people practice dark arts, the summoning of demons, and the worship of Satan, or the like. Most notably in the possession cases, the person has no memory of the events that take place. For example, they will speak with a voice that is not theirs or act in a manner completely unlike themselves, and later when questioned they have no memory, or feel they were pushed into a role as witness of events as if they are watching a movie. A demonic can inject thoughts into a person that they can consider as their own. These are usually negative against the person, to break down their will, making them more susceptible to further demonic control, but they can also direct these thoughts outwardly. In the 'Devil made me do it' excuse, we skirt the line between mental and spiritual. In a mental illness (with psychosis) or a demonic attack, the factors the person are experiencing are very real to them. The dividing line is scientific method, where an experiment must be replicated. Science has done experiments again and again to establish a fact, while the Church also has its own methods that have been worked and reworked in establishing the beliefs and methods used for all these years, and still in use today. A person's history plays a part in the whole of a person. How the form, and create a belief system, and interact or see the world around them. A jilted person will be cautious, an abused person more sensitive to a person who is abused etc. We find in some of these cases of murder, that it was done, (for) Satan, requiring a sacrifice, or payment for a barter. Faust style.

Ramirez apparently believed he was protected by Satan himself. Is this unique?

For a time, yes. The god-like complex is being brought forward if it be a mental divergent or belief that they are under the protection and service of a higher power than themselves. In a mental illness this will continue until a force stops or thwarts it, in a spiritual, it will expose itself in the failings around them. A person under the influence of a or multiple (the usual case) demons may act following the thoughts, this will be unsustainable in the long run, as the entity will not stop in its appetite, and its destruction of the person, to the point of suicide.

I understand you are experienced in the topic of exorcism. Please elaborate.

As with any vocation, there is an amount of study, and dedication to be apt. In the Church, the exorcist is in the minor orders, but I will be honest that it really isn't a focus in most seminaries. I discussed this vocation with my higher ups early in my holy orders, was evaluated inside and outside the church, and was given the green light to go forward based on my qualifications, temperament, understanding and ability to sustain such a difficult vocation. One thing I did learn while studying under my mentor and other exorcists, is there is no halfway in and halfway out to this. Each time stepping into that role, it is one of the most important times for both myself, and the client. People have died during exorcisms, priests have died, or been permanently retired from the struggle. One very experienced person handling a case against a bruja in Mexico, was taken out of working for over two years, this is not a job for the faint of heart.

Many priests and pastors choose not to take this on for various reasons. Once the decision was made, then it became my job, to learn from the best, and never ever stop learning. I have a multi-cultural approach to the world because, one cultures myths, demons, and rites, do not end at their countries border. So, to best help any client, I have studied and continue to do so, daily. Study though is not enough. It is one thing to have faith, it is completely another to take it out of the box and stand on it alone. I have experiences helping across the country and conferring internationally, and as long as the Lord grants me health and breath I will serve the Church, and those in need.

In my study of psychology history, it seems the concept of possession has been used as an excuse for a number of other issues, such as mental illness, organic disorder or even simply having unpopular beliefs. Do you agree with this?

As evolving science and understanding has progressed through the ages, I agree with your question, that sometimes the possession or the devil inside of someone, has been used as a weapon of control, subjugation or to ostracize (and in some cases pursue and kill) someone. The gods of one culture becoming the demons of the next idea. That being used as a misdiagnosis exists, as I also believe there are cases where the diagnosis is mental illness, where it is really, at least in some part a spiritual attack. This makes the union the full gamut of our resources necessary.

What's the Church's position on that?

The Church position is as stated. We study and train in all aspects of the religious and at least a cursory understanding of psychology, medical, etc. and we have access to highly trained individuals and experts in their prospective fields to aid us in substantiating or dismissing the evidence presented in a case.

What is the Church's, and your, opinion on mental illness today as it relates to the concept of possession?

Mental Illness. As I have stated the Church, requires the evaluation of a person to proceed with an exorcism. This is important for the person, the priest, and the Church. When we talk about the attacks of the demonic, they can not only mimic the symptoms of a mental illness, they can also hide behind them. In some cases, the two (mental illness and possession) are not mutually exclusive. Care and compassion for the client can come in many forms of support. The necessary evaluation and review from the bishop are required in proceeding forward. Having these layers, offers the best possible care for the person who, is experiencing things that are not the common everyday plight of modern man. But it is for some. A percentage of individuals are suffering from some level of spiritual attacks above the norm of temptations which are the most common form.

Is there a "placebo effect" in performing an exorcism on a person who could be mentally ill?

A tricky question. The placebo effect, seems to carry an amount of success in most every situation that it has been used. Council, blessings, and encouragement yes can help in many situations. In an exorcism, Father Gabriele Amorth stated that he never saw an exorcism hurt anyone, meaning that he did exorcisms that could have been conducted for that effect, yes. In my opinion, I would not conduct the major rite of the Church when it was not needed. There is an exorcist priest who made it a point to go to prisons, and found many of the imprisoned where, actually possessed, and conducted exorcisms to liberate them. Now for the mentally ill. It is a standard of the Church and my own practice to evaluate for mental illness. I personally have three psych on staff that I can call and refer the client, to be evaluated. A particular case locally, the female described many of the things that could possibly be of spiritual nature and was convinced that she was being tormented by the demonic, by using the access to psych, we discovered that she was experiencing a medicine induced psychosis and we were able to get her to the help she needed, medical, not clergy. But it was reaching out to us that was able to get her to where she needed. I embrace psych and medical as partners in my ministry. I always rely on someone experienced in their particular field, as they do for me in mine. I would not recommend an exorcism for the mentally ill as a placebo, as it could exacerbate the condition, rather that provide relief.

How much training on clinical psychology would a member of the clergy need to have to consider and recognize the role of mental illness in a person seeking an exorcism?

Some priests are trained psychologists, not usually, they have trained to be priests. In this vocation (exorcist), there is a need for the basic understanding and aware of all the possible things that could be in play other than the spiritual component. The role is the ultimate skeptic, yet with full sympathy and compassion of the situation. Hence, we always bring in trained psychologists for the clinical diagnosis, that will establish or debunk, mental illness or other maladies like brain damage, drug psychosis, social problems, or malingering.

Could you discuss your personal history with rites of exorcism?

We can discuss this one at another time.

What about follow-up in these cases?

Follow up, after care, is hugely important to me. Scripture reads in Matt 12-45 and again in Luke 11-26, that when a spirit departs, it can return with seven more, worse than the original. This is a true statement. (AUTHOR NOTE: stated in Matthew, "brings with it seven other spirits more wicked than itself") That is not the only reason after care is so important. A person that has been through any kind of trauma, or situation, it takes time and understanding to aid long term recovery. That is the goal, long term, recovery. So, it is never a one and done. The council and prayer or referring to mental health and talking with the family are in play. Using this approach you have a team of loved ones, friends and professionals doing the best they can for the client. I look at the ministry at time like a light house, we have repaired the boat and they are sailing again, and I keep the lighthouse going, giving them support, confidence and help when they need it.

Is there conflict within the Church in the proper procedure and consideration of someone or their family seeking an exorcism?

In what I consider most cases, it is usually the family member or friend that notices the changes in a person. Then they are the ones that seek inquiries or care for the person. There is a cross denominational, and cross-cultural need for the Rite of Exorcism. Every culture that has come into existence, has had a belief in, or way to deal with the negative spiritual side of life. Different churches and cultures have their own form of how they deal or do not deal with these cases. A well-established intake is necessary and involving the family, is so beneficial for the immediate and long-term success of any intervention.

How, in your opinion, have popular culture and films/TV affected the field of exorcism?

Pop culture has caused a resurgence of interest in the topic. This, I feel has been a double-edged sword. The illumination of a topic that has been mostly suppressed in the west, is good. For example, Italy has requests for 500,000 exorcisms a year. In the older countries of the world, the spiritual side of existence has long been embraced as the norm. Pop Culture has breached that topic, yet, it has caused a landslide of misinformation, and gave rise to a subculture of fans, who, untrained attempt to make contact or proceed forward as someone who seeing a few episodes of a ghost hunter show, go out on their own, giving themselves the title (ghost hunter, investigator, paranormal expert etc.). Even so much so, as passing for someone who can remedy the activity people are having, which, usually makes it much worse, like kicking a hornet's nest. Also charging for services. I had a case, where someone offered to exorcise the home (minor rite) for the sum of 3000 dollars, which he was giving them a discount at that price. I believe stated a number of these investigators and hunters, end up needing clergy or psychological intervention themselves after attempting this for various amounts of time.

Father Casey hoped this opened a line of dialogue. He graciously offered an ongoing conversation and I'm thrilled he's provided this small glimpse into this fascinating dimension. I must admit this exchange simply sparked my interest in this topic, which considers a connection between the possessed and the predatory.

EVIL AS OPPOSED TO MENTAL ILLNESS

Many laypeople consider the most predatory and violent of criminals to have some sort of mental illness. While this is a dicey subject when brought into the courtroom, particularly when it bleeds into the realm of exculpatory factors, people often separate the possibility of insanity, a legal term, which might include psychosis and personality disorders, by describing the offender as simply "evil."

Is this a different concept from descriptions of antisocial personality disorder, or sociopath? Is it different than a psychopath? A sadist? Most of the worst violent serial sexual offenders or serial murderers would describe an obsession, a compulsion that they simply are unable to resist.

Are they possessed by evil?

In the book, *The Devil is Afraid of Me*, chronicling the life and work of quite possibly the world's most famous exorcist, Father Gabrielle Amorth, (referenced by Father Casey) Father Marcello Stanzione discusses The Devil. The Enemy, as he's also called, goes by many names. But by any name, The Evil One is often the totem by which people refer to the concept of "evil."

HUMAN BEINGS, MURDER AND DUALISM

Father Stanzione acknowledges the danger of the concept of dualism, which refers to "the theory that there are two conflicting powers, good and evil, in the universe." The light and the darkness. This dualism or "duality," is often pointed to in the makeup of humans and their psychological construction. There are those who believe both these parts to the human mind are essential.

My interviews with a serial killer detailed in my last book brought out his belief that human beings have a primitive part of their psyches, a place that a person likely would not be the same after he visited. A child therapist I once presented with was an expert in therapy with children suffering from Reactive Attachment Disorder. She once described some patients reverting to a "primitive" state, pawing at the ground and growling like an animal. These stories reminded me of accounts of serial killer Gerald Stano, described as a child, functioning at an "animalistic level" when removed from his nightmarish upbringing before adoption.

All of these seem like examples of the human mind reverting to an extreme level most people don't believe they are capable of.

Father Stanzione argues that, to say "evil does not exist is an unjust trivialization of evil, and evil is never trivial." He reminds that "not all evil is done by man; indeed, originally man committed evil, but he did it through a suggestion that came from a distance." He also clarifies that this "does not authorize an abandonment of responsibility."

This describes evil as an objective consistency, or that "the demon is an evil inclination in the heart of man." He references Protestant theologians who "affirm that the demons are mental structures." He concludes, then that "if, in the heart of man, there is, even from birth, an evil inclination, then this inclination comes from God."

Father Casey spoke with me about cases of "spiritual attack" he'd consulted on recently. He referenced the huge number of reported requests made in Italy in recent years, and said, "That number is correct. The rest of the world does embrace the idea and fact of spiritual warfare, as a daily part of life. Here in the west, it has been suppressed and not even preached upon in most churches. You cannot read the New Testament without the reality of Jesus ministry of exorcism. Even as medical psych and all forms of understanding have evolved with new understanding, the reality of that spiritual war, is still underpinning our unseen reality."

This discussion suggests, to me, a confluence of the concepts of possession and mental illness. I do not know the origin of the psychosis that took over the woman's mind I spoke about at the beginning of this chapter, leading her to commit murder, an unimaginable act by those that knew her. As well, I cannot explain the concepts of demonic possession or spiritual attack and the resulting demands made of exorcists like Father Casey and Father Amorth.

Are they one and the same?

The very image on this book's cover that artist David Van Gough created of a familiar figure of our culture peering into the mirror and gazing at his most possessed, demonic, evil self, can be interpreted as the ultimate in mental illness, or the horror of possession, but is unquestionably an example of the dualism of the human mind.

REFERENCES

American Psychiatric Association. (2013). *Diagnostic and statistical manual of mental disorders, 5th edition.* Arlington, VA: American Psychiatric Publishing.

Amorth, Fr. Gabriele & Stanzione, Fr. Marcello. (2019). *The devil is afraid of me. The life and work of the world's most famous exorcist.* Manchester, NH: Sophia Institute Press.

Bishop, James. (2018, January 8). 9 facts about exorcism & demonic possession. *Reasonsforjesus.com.*

Crary, David. (2020, October 31). Exorcism: Increasingly frequent, including after US protests. *AP.* Apnews.com.

Deanna Laney out of mental institution. (2012, May 24). *KLTV.* www.kltv.com.

English Standard Version Bible. (2001). Matthew 12:45. ESV Online. htts://esvliteralword.

McCalope, Michelle. (2001, September 20). Doctor: Texas mother saw 'Satan'. *The Washington Post.* www.washingtonpost.com.

Request an Exorcism- The archdiocese of Washington. (N.D.) https://adw.org/about-us/resources/.

Resnick, M.D., Phillip J. (2011, March 31). (video presentation) *The Andrea Yates case: insanity on trial*. UNM Department of Psychiatry/ Law school. You Tube.

Springer, John. (2004, April 1). In interview, mother details delusions that spurred her to kill her sons. *CNN.com*, Court TV.

The Exorcist. (1973). William Peter Blatty/William Friedkin. Hoya Productions.

United States Conference of Catholic Bishops. (N.D.) https://www.usccb.org/prayer-and-worship/sacraments-and-sacramentals/sacramentals-blessings/exorcism.

CHAPTER 11

Teaching Serial Murder, and a Legacy

"The more I study this subject, the more I realize how little I know"

-Dr. Steven Egger

Dr. Clyde Snow, who helped ID Gacy victims.
(Oklahoma City, USA. David Longstreet/AP/Shutterstock.)

When I bring Pogo the Clown into the classroom, one of the first questions I get is, "how can you possibly have that in your house?" Between this and Richard Speck's autograph and black cats, I obviously don't believe in bad luck. There are some great stories out there of Pogo owners that do. The bottom line is artifacts such as this generally start some great conversation and discussion.

I should point this fact out though… one of the most recent incidences of this exchange happened one evening in March 2020. After class, a student shyly but with concern asked me about the evil energy I was toying with in utilizing these art pieces as "show and tell" items. She said I might be tempting the fates a bit. I said she's probably right and hopefully my house won't be on fire when I get home.

It wasn't, but it seemed the world was. In a matter of days, the COVID-19 pandemic hit, and the planet was closed down for "two weeks to flatten the curve." It seems that it's been longer. At any rate, that night was literally the last time in-person classes seemed the same, and Mr. Pogo just could be laughing while he peers over my shoulder. Or maybe it was a coincidence.

TEACHING SERIAL MURDER

Previous chapters of this book have mentioned my first book, *The Psychopathology of Serial Murder: A Theory of Violence*. Much of this book was created through the research for my master's degree thesis on Serial Murder psychology, a topic I felt was underdeveloped in the 1990s. In 1992 I took my first graduate level-course towards that forensic psychology degree and was blessed to meet international serial murder expert Steven Egger, who would eventually become my mentor, colleague, and friend.

Dr. Egger eventually asked me to make presentations to his classes after my graduation on the book material. One semester in which I'd already made a presentation, Dr. Egger took ill, and I was asked to teach the remainder of his course in the emergency. Long story short, I eventually took over Dr. Egger's class at Sangamon State University, now the University of Illinois Springfield. Somehow, I've managed to stay there over 20 years, teaching both Serial Murder and Psychology of the Offender in various semesters.

I really enjoy talking about my books with people, and I think the most common topic is how they fit into my classroom. Speaking with different serial murder afficionados, I can't say how many times I've heard, "you teach a university class on serial killers? I'd LOVE to take a course like that!" And to be honest, over the years, the class has been routinely full, and along with the usual Psychology or Criminal Justice Majors, there's those people from every other discipline and interest group and all types of people who simply love to talk about this fascinating topic. The subject definitely drives the class popularity.

I've considered my time teaching this subject matter a gift. I've continued to research the topic, received training from terrific sources all around the country, and been able to learn something new from the incredibly bright and fertile minds of students that's passed through my classroom. I'm going to say the students that sign up for Serial Murder or Psychology of the Offender tend to be just a bit more motivated than your average student, as often the class fills to the max head count and many of the students have already read my books along with many others by the time they sit in their first class with me.

While not routine, it's unforeseen… when another bright mind throws me another curve, asks a question I'd never thought of, or comes up with a paper or a report that I could see finding its way into publication. I'm just not surprised by what they are capable of.

LETTERS AND PAINTINGS IN THE CLASSROOM

Recently, I provided some commentary for a series of podcasts entitled *Killers Vault*, which were generated by a vast collection of serial killer correspondence to a couple of collectors from the likes of Richard Ramirez, John Wayne Gacy, David Alan Gore and Fred Waterfield, The Toolbox Killers Roy Norris and Lawrence Bittaker and Gerard Schaefer. It was an interesting take as the simple concept presented the dramatic reading of these killers' personally written letters by Eric Roberts, moderated by Law & Order alum Elisabeth Rohm, and discussed by Dr. Katherine Ramsland, collector Robert Webb and me.

These conversations really were a fascinating look at some of the things these people said on paper when "speaking" to people they trusted, people considered friends. It's a rare look at raw information.

I do like to bring letters into the classroom as they often represent thoughts by the authors that might be as close to honest as possible. Of course, serial killers lie. Of course, they try to shock and influence a reader sometimes. But there are times you can parse through the noise and pick out some actual self-reflection, some honest opinion, and some useful information.

Paintings, too, can provide a peek into a person's head, sometimes. Like letters, you should dismiss products that appear to be produced to shock the viewer. But as has been studied for many years within clinical psychology, examination of paintings and artwork by brain disordered individuals has often glean some information and insight. I spoke of the use of paintings in the classroom in Chapter 1, but I'll re-state that their use as a tool to engage students has been remarkably effective over the years.

Letter from Dennis Rader/ BTK. (Author photo.)

GUEST SPEAKERS

One method of teaching I've had for class is the use of guest speakers. I've always felt it's cruel and unusual punishment to make students listen to my voice for 3 hours, so in the interest of breaking things up, film, audio, student presentations and the occasional guest speaker has been a welcome change of pace.

Here's a word of caution for the would-be teacher looking to use guest speakers: It's way more difficult than it sounds.

I thought the hard part would be to find the right person. Oh, it's hard alright, but bringing in guest speakers has seemed like the most difficult thing in the world some-times. I've had speakers cancel last-minute or simply not show up, had speakers com-pletely present a different topic than we had agreed upon, some disappear from any sort of contact forever after agreeing to present, and present the same material to essentially the same students in another instructor's class (this is filed under, "stealing another instructor's speaker"). I went to one speaker's house who'd been painfully injured in an accident and brought him to class in a wheelchair. Huge points to him for gutting that one out.

Of course, the seasoned instructor learns very quickly to prepare a full back-up presen-tation for a night that a speaker is scheduled. This technique is also effective in pro-tection against the inevitable, insidious, looming equipment failure that all instructors eventually encounter.

The only thing more disappointing than a speaker who doesn't show is to lose a trea-sured speaker you have used for years. Some stars at this assignment for me have been Cathy Clevenger, a brilliant presenter on the ins and outs of Reactive Attachment Dis-order, high-risk children, and therapy with this population. She was an indispensable asset for many years until she moved on to take her talents to another geographic area. Cathy was a bit too valuable to cage in.

Another great speaker was John Borowski, a Chicago-area movie producer, author and serial killer expert, whose relentless research methods has made his documentaries and books must- have items in any afficionado's collection. His stories mesmerized the students, and they loved his appearances.

And another I must mention is Rick Wiese, a retired Springfield Police Department officer who had an old personal case that he worked involving an offender who stalked young girls for kidnapping and "keeping" them as a stolen "partner." This case was full of the psychological drama over the years involving the case. His personal professional experience was so valuable in a Psychology of the Offender class and kept students on the edge of their seats. This is another speaker able to impart knowledge from experience on to students that they could never access in a book.

Speakers like this are irreplaceable. Find a way to bribe them to keep them from getting away.

STUDENTS SPEAK

Thinking back to my first class as a teacher of Serial Murder, I remember a student that I became friends with, and we kept in touch for several years. She's since become a Ph.D. and a successful professor in her own right, and it was nice to have been part of that early influence. A few years later, a friend I grew up with asked me to speak with his niece, who was considering a career with the FBI but was tentative about embarking down that road. I tried to give her all the insight and encouragement possible at the time. When she contacted me many years later to tell me about her successful career with the Bureau, it was gratifying.

There's a lot of reasons students take classes involving murder and mayhem.

A young woman currently serving in the U.S. military and former student, Amy Greenan, commented about taking these classes:

> I have always found the psychology, criminology, and criminal justice fields fascinating. I guess I am drawn to figuring out puzzles, along with the intrigue of trying to understand what on Earth went wrong to make some people tick the way they do. My interest in these subjects have led me to obtaining a bachelor's degree in psychology and Criminal Justice. I plan to accomplish my master's degree next so I can finally land an amazing career working for the Federal Government as a Forensic Psychologist, Criminal Profiler, detective, or anything in relation to those lines of work. Throughout my educational journey, I was lucky enough to attend Professor Giannangelo's courses, *Psychology of the Offender* and *Serial Murder*. Not to discredit any of my other instructors, they were all wonderful, but his courses were my favorite. We learned about the factors involved in becoming a successful

detective or criminal profiler, such as the capability to proficiently identify whether the individual is a psychopath or sociopath, Modus Operandi, signature, trophies, how to lure a criminal into a trap, and many other crucial skills required in closing a criminal case. As a Forensic Psychologist being knowledgeable of all of this is also beneficial to identify potential suspects for law enforcement through interrogations and interviews. We were able to analyze paintings, correspondence, and other murderabilia from well-known criminals that I found very interesting. The subject matter we covered in professor Giannangelo's courses was so captivating that I feel I will always be able to retain it and if I am lucky, be able to utilize it in my next career!

Another talented woman, a former student aspiring to a federal career, Eva Santucci, said:

I think one thing that really stood out to me about taking your psychology of the offender course was how valuable it is to have a professor who has lived experience in law enforcement. I have found, quite often, that forensic psychology courses tend to be taught by people who have been more involved in the academic side of the discipline than the law enforcement side, which can lead to a lack of understanding about how well the concepts discussed carry over into real world application. However, you have first-hand knowledge of how these concepts present in the field. The fact that you are able to offer insight on interviewing an offender based on first-hand knowledge, for example, is both engaging and relevant for someone who hopes to enter the field and conduct the same type of interviews someday.

Having law enforcement experience also means that you are able to explain not only what the concepts discussed are, but also why they matter. In *Psychology of the Offender* we discussed how the material could be interpreted across a wide variety of systems, including legal proceedings, law enforcement, and public perception. Having a professor who is able to explain the role these systems regarding mental illness, offenders, and their traits, leads to a more nuanced understanding of the topic as a whole. Additionally, discussing how the perspective of legal and law enforcement systems varies in regard to offender psychology is absolutely imperative, as each system will view the offender through its own lens, and may present or emphasize only the information that is relevant through said lens if discussed in isolation.

And another former student, Keith Hauter, has gone on to a career as a Trooper with the Illinois State Police. His comments:

> I was 28 years old when I walked into Steve's *Serial Murder* class on the campus at the University of Illinois Springfield. I didn't know what to expect, sitting in a room full of teenagers, but after the first session I was hooked. I became obsessed with serial murderers and could not put down different books I would rent weekly at my local library. I became hooked on names like Charles Manson, John Wayne Gacy and Ted Bundy. At the end of the semester, I needed more. The way Steve taught was consuming and I could not get enough. I found myself having deep conversations during our breaks with Steve about different serial killer personalities. I completed *Psychology of the Offender* and *Serial Murder* in my senior year and based on the volume of information I obtained through the courses, I can truly say the information I obtained has helped me to understand the how and why when it relates to criminals. Understanding the criminal mind is no easy task, however over the years Steve has been very successful. Teaching is even more of a difficult task and Steve does an outstanding job. Serving as an Illinois State Trooper, I have been able to take the information from the courses and apply it in everyday interactions with the public.
>
> It is easy to testify to what you see in an interaction, but it is equally, if not more important to be able to explain why someone does something. Understanding a person's mindset and personality helps me to comprehend what type of person I am dealing with on a traffic stop. Being able to understand the difference between someone who is a sociopath vs. psychopath is also very important. This information is very valuable in my work as a trooper.
>
> Most importantly, when evaluating an instructor, it is important for me to believe what someone is telling me is the truth and not something they simply read from a book or watched on television. Based on first-hand experience with dangerous minded individuals, I can say Steve is hands down, one of the top subject matter experts in his field. He has interviewed serial killers and violent offenders and enjoys passing along his experiences to his students. Steve's publishings are intoxicating, and I cannot wait for the next one to be released.

THE SUBJECT CONTINUES TO CHANGE

I think the biggest issue within the subject of teaching Serial Murder is the need to evolve and learn with the times. When I began study of the subject in the 70s and 80s, the vast majority of the available expert material came from a handful of groundbreaking researchers like Eric Hickey, Steve Egger, Fox & Levin and a few others. As well were the valuable interviews and research conducted by the early pioneers of the FBI Behavioral Analysis Unit (BAU) like John Douglas, Roy Hazelwood, Robert Ressler, and Ann Burgess to name a few. Stories related to the early BAU research have been brought to our living rooms by the Netflix series *Mindhunter*, providing some historical context to the early days of studying serial murder.

"Mindhunter" (Season 1) TV Series- 2017.
(Merrick Morton/Netflix/Kobal/Shutterstock).

The colleges and universities that offer majors in Forensic Psychology and classes on Serial Murder have exploded in recent years. University instructors routinely have the available resources to take ongoing training which offers an opportunity to increase skills in the classroom as well as on the technical side. They are of course valuable and worthwhile. But it should be remembered that a topic like Serial Murder can evolve and turn on a dime. If one wants to present Forensic Psychology/Psychology of the Offender/Serial Murder, they must not only be aware of the volume of relevant cases in history but keep up with the new cases that pop up every day... or the discovery of cold cases like Little or Joe DeAngelo, who were successful serial killers for decades without our slightest idea. Cold cases are being looked at with more skills, more technology, and a far deeper knowledge base than ever before and are unearthing old serial murder cases and victims of known cases seemingly every week.

As well, a teacher in this genre needs to be aware of topics within the subject, such as current research, statistics and trends, comparative theory, historical context, relevant developing theory such as biological analysis... the list is endless. And just when we think we have heard everything, serial murderers exhibit new or unusual behaviors, such as the unexplained serial bombings of a Mark Conditt, the seemingly random shootings of Howell Donaldson or the completely bizarre, unheard-of acts of Lawrence Paul Mills III of Garden City, MI. Mills may be the first known serial killer who used his car as the murder weapon, soliciting women for sex in the Detroit area, then running them down and fleeing in up to 5 separate incidents, at least 2 fatal.

Fortunately, there's a myriad of training opportunities open to researchers in this field. In recent years I've attended training and conferences put on by BAU legend Ann Burgess and pioneers Fox and Levin at Northeastern University and the AHRG in Boston, another at New Haven CT /Yale Campus by Forensics legend Dr. Henry Lee and an outstanding annual Homicide conference presented in Green Bay WI, by Northeast Wisconsin Technical College. Former Corrections Officer, author and Conference Founder Steve Daniels, discussed the Green Bay event:

> 27 years ago, the Public Safety Training Division, Northeast Wisconsin Technical College started an annual homicide training conference to offer investigators, and allied professionals state-of-the-art information. Each year, the conference selects a different focus with the central theme always being homicide. Presentations were offered by speakers from the FBI, RCMP, ATF, DEA, plus local, state agencies and retired professionals.

> Annual sessions have focused on gangs and murder, domestic terrorism and homicide, as well as poisoning, criminal snipers, homicidal arson, murder in the LGBT community and so much more. Techniques such as interviewing skills, use of DNA and genealogy, digital investigations plus more. Local case studies are often interwoven into sessions, as well as cases of national and international scope, such as Lake/Ng, the serial killing pair from California. Waco. Oklahoma City bombing, plus a plethora of others. The conference has offered CCTV hook-ups with the local maximum security prison so attendees could interview persons incarcerated for murder. This was extremely well received by attendees. Family members of murder

victims have served as presenters to offer the perspective of those who have suffered immensely.

Investigators and homicide researchers have utilized many techniques such as the ones listed above. Researchers and practitioners gather after the sessions for "brain-picking" sessions and networking among attendees. Presenters often join the mini gatherings after training day is over. I have found, in my work that the information received was invaluable to dealing with violent offenders.

This event is an excellent example of the ongoing training so beneficial to teaching courses within Criminology, particularly those involving homicide.

Participating in Guest lectures at these conferences also improve the instructor's depth in the field along with the knowledge gained by listening and networking with colleagues. Presenting pushes the instructors to sharpen their own expertise and command of the field and hones the ability to impart these concepts to others. I've found making presentations at various events to law enforcement officers and personnel at Police academy settings as well as academic environments is a learning experience for me in every case. I'm looking forward to making a planned video presentation at a Serial Murder Conference in England in late 2022, another new experience.

LEARNING AND TEACHING THROUGH SUBJECT INTERVIEWS

Of course, I've already discussed this point in its own chapter, but I cannot overstate the value of the one-on one learning process in conducting personal interviews. My small experience in the activity pales in comparison to the Robert Resslers and John Douglasses and Roy Hazelwoods who have had the opportunity to learn from killer interviews at length. Even so, the interviews I've conducted have been wildly useful in my subsequent time teaching.

A LEGEND IN THE FIELD OFFERS PERSPECTIVE

I've known a few other individuals that have taught Serial Murder or Forensic Psychology at the University level. There's probably no better expert on the topic of writing and teaching about these subjects today than Dr. Katherine Ramsland. Doctor Ramsland has taught both topics for many years, has written over 60 books on the subject and is likely at the top of anyone's list of experts in this field. Her 2016 work *Confession of a Serial Killer: The Untold Story of Dennis Rader the BTK Killer* is a course in Serial Murder in itself.

I asked Dr. Ramsland for some insight on her experience and methods on teaching these subjects and she generously provided the following essay:

Teaching a course about serial killers

Dr. Katherine Ramsland

The most persistent challenge when introducing the subject of serial killers is to sift through media hype and error. I start with the most prevalent myths so my students quickly discover that what they think they know from fiction, podcasts, news reports, and documentaries is likely to be incomplete, even flawed. I've worked with many producers. They have to pitch ideas to get network support. This means they create their hook before fully exploring the data and have taken a position they must now support. So, the same stories, including errors, get recycled to the point that they seem like irrefutable facts.

I show how some of the myths derive from claims made by FBI profilers during the 1980s based on poorly designed research. At the time, they'd interviewed more serial killers than most, endowing the agents with authority, but their sample was small, selective, and unrepresentative. It should never have become the ground for generalizable truths. So, I spend time on how and why their limited findings still permeate media as "the facts."

Students are often surprised to learn that we've documented several thousand serial killers around the world. They've generally heard of about two-dozen. I show them that current research databases reach well beyond what law enforcement has collected. The diversity in this population makes it impossible to provide a generic serial killer "profile."

Then there's the definition. It's tough to convey how this has evolved, because some think a definition is simply a fact. The criteria for a serial killer began to form for law enforcement during the 1970s, with the FBI's budding Behavioral Science Unit (now the BAU) leading the way. Initially, these agents had designated three or more victims in three or more locations.

These killings were considered separate but linked events, with a "cooling off" period between them. The requirement for three locations (which fails to fit those who used a single location) dropped out for *The Crime Classification Manual* (1992), but the "emotional cooling off period" was retained. Some criminologists argued for including motivation, which distinguished a specific type of offender from multiple repeat murderers who wouldn't qualify as serial killers (e.g., gangs and organized crime syndicates). In addition, some thought the concept of "cooling off" was vague.

To address these concerns, in 2005 the FBI organized a symposium for law enforcement, academicians, cops, and clinicians. The participants agreed that the lowest possible minimum number of victims would offer the greatest flexibility for law enforcement and still be useful for research. Since serial killers had diverse motives (e.g., power, thrill, anger, profit, mission, sexual satisfaction), it seemed expedient to leave this out. In 2008, the FBI announced the new definition for serial murder: *The unlawful killing of two or more victims by the same offender(s), in separate events.* Not all law enforcement agencies or researchers accept this, especially outside the U.S., but the Agency tends to set the standard. Yet I still see media quote the 1980s definition.

Once the basics are established, I tackle the question I'm asked most often: "Does life experiences make someone a serial killer, or are they born this way?" Such a query contains two flawed assumptions, notably that:

1) "serial killer" is a distinct type of criminal category that confers upon these offenders distinct similarities in personality, MO, and motivation; and

2) we can effectively calculate a clear ratio between the influence of nature and nurture.

If we use the FBI's current stance, what defines a serial killer is a specific behavior:

Having killed two or more victims in at least two distinct events. No other personality or behavioral characteristics place all serial killers into this criminological category. We do have typologies, typically based on motivation, but there's little agreement on which typology is most useful. We find a

lot of variation in this offender population, from a range of motives, back-
grounds, ages, and lifestyles, to differences in physiology, sex, mental state,
and perceptions that influence reasoning and decisions.

Among the approaches I use in my course to address nature vs. nurture
is a theory proposed by neuropsychologist Debra Niehoff. She's reviewed
the most significant literature about the interplay of genes and the environment in the development of violent behavior, and she finds that each factor
modifies the other in different ways for different people at different stages
throughout their lifespans. That's complex! Each person uniquely processes
a given situation, and some gravitate toward violence. This might be defensive or aggressive, psychotic or psychopathic, reactive or predatory, to name
some possibilities. Any factor – abuse, neglect, deviance, bullying, humiliation – might have different influences on different people, and new experiences can modify perceptions either positively or negatively. One person
with a brain abnormality might become violent, but others with the same
disorder might not, and yet others with no such disorder might turn to violence for other reasons. How each person sorts it out and manages his or
her situation depends on a unique interplay of external and internal factors.

In other words, for any given person, we don't know how much of their
development into serial killers is due to something in their physiology vs.
something from their environment. We know it's both, but we can't accurately calculate which has more influence. In that case, we also don't know
if an ability to calculate this ratio will be particularly meaningful. We hope
it will be, and those in neurocriminology and neuropsychology have such
goals. But we're not there yet.

Despite its lack of a simple formula, I prefer to provide this open-ended
approach to understanding the developmental trajectory of specific cases. I
begin with some of the youngest extreme offenders, both mass and serial
killers. Their lives have often been picked apart, so it's easy to look at the early development and focus on vulnerabilities, fantasies, and trigger points for
violence. The students begin to see the features these cases have in common,
especially such aspects as disorders, psychopathy, narcissistic entitlement,
and paraphilias.

Then we move on to adult offenders, according to motivational categories. I dispense with the idea that only a sexually compelled repeat offender can be classified as a serial killer. I identify multiple other motives. I also look at historical serial killers like Jack the Ripper, Belle Gunness, Joseph Vacher, Leonarda Cianciulli, and H. H. Holmes. Then I'll cover the typical killers: Bundy, Gacy, Kemper, Wuornos, and Dahmer, as well as team killers. I spend more time on Dennis "BTK" Rader, because I've worked with him for a decade to analyze the important influences. He's an outlier for many notions about serial killers, so it's beneficial for students to study his case in-depth. In addition, I'll describe serial killers who aren't well known. For all of them, I spend a lot of time on their developmental psychology.

Finally, I wrap up with the latest neuroscience of violence, pointing out implications and treatments for different types of violence. Dr. Adriane Raine found brain deficits in violent individuals – specifically in the limbic system (emotional center) and the prefrontal cortex. These deficits might influence certain people to be impulsive, fearless, less responsive to aversive stimulation, and less able to make appropriate decisions about aggression toward others. Or… they might not.

I end the course with something lighter: serial killer culture. I bring in calendars, aprons, trading cards and other items that collectors value. I discuss groupies, podcasts, murderabilia sites, conferences, movies, and other items to show the enormous interest serial killers have attracted. It's a way to bring students down from the intensity but also to talk about social influences on serial killer celebrity.

Overall, I present serial killers as a complex group of offenders for which we benefit more from detailed case analysis than from statistics that hide their diversity and place them into oversimplified categories. And we're still learning.

A LEGACY

I've mentioned Dr. Steven Egger a few times in this book. As I've stated, he was a mentor and a dear friend for many years. As I've written this book as a general reflection on years of studying and teaching serial murder, I'd be remiss if I didn't mention Dr. Egger specifically, and his role in this.

Dr. Egger served in the U.S. Army and was a Police Officer, a homicide investigator, expert consultant, and law enforcement academy director. He earned his Ph.D. at Sam Houston State in Criminal Justice where he completed the first dissertation on serial murder in the world. Steve taught at the University of Illinois Springfield and at the University of Houston for over 25 years. He lectured internationally as well as participating in the landmark FBI serial murder symposium. He was project director of the Homicide Assessment and Lead Tracking System (HALT) for the state of New York. HALT, which was the first statewide computerized system to track and identify serial murderers, has been a blueprint for future systems. His ground-breaking books in the study of serial murder, development of a serial murderer database, interviews with serial killers like Henry Lee Lucas and John Wayne Gacy and tireless research efforts in the field left a legend that's tough to follow.

I took my first Serial Murder class as a graduate student with Dr. Egger in 1992. This was when the subject was even more in its infancy than it is today but was still as intoxicating. Dr. Egger was an accomplished and respected international expert, and it was a pleasure to learn from him. I and other students considered it a privilege to sit in his classes.

I particularly remember his first discussion on profiling, a topic we can never leave out of the subject of Serial Murder, whether its 1992 or 2022. He detailed the BAU's analysis of the murders committed by The Vampire killer, Richard Chase in California in 1977-78. Observations such as the likelihood the killer was a disorganized offender and probably displayed overt mental illness given it appeared he walked to the various murder sites and left the crime scenes an uncovered mess, including a yogurt cup that blood had been drank from, were intuitive but accurate. Profiler opinions that the killer was likely clearly a suspicious looking disheveled mess added to the picture. Looking back 30 years, this profile wasn't exactly hocus-pocus, but it was a small sample of how the subject hooked me. Dr. Egger also mentioned that you will often hear this example as a successful piece of profiling, but rarely will hear about the failures, a caveat I always never fail to mention. Dr. Egger always brought a heavy dose of skepticism to the table.

I took over Dr. Egger's Serial Murder class when he fell ill for a while and eventually moved. I was glad that he resumed his teaching later. But I must acknowledge that everything I've reflected on in this book, from personal study and growth as well as experiences in the classroom, started with Dr. Steven Egger and his Serial Murder class, and this is a legacy that has and will endure within the study of this provocative and intriguing subject.

REFERENCES

Fernandez, Manny; Saul, Stephanie & Healy, Jack. (2018, March 21). Who is Mark Conditt, the suspected Austin serial bomber? *The New York Times.* www.nytimes.com.

Giannangelo, Stephen J. (1996). *The Psychopathology of Serial Murder: A Theory of Violence.* Westport, CT. Praeger.

Killers Vault. (podcasts, Season 1). New York. Killer Bunny Entertainment/ Surveillance TV.

Marquis, Erin. (2020, May 16). This might be the first serial killer to use a car as the murder weapon. *Jalopnik.* https://jalopnik.com.

O'Connell, Mary. (2020, October 7). Accused Seminole Heights killer Howell Donaldson III to have four separate trials. *ABC Action News/ WFTS Tampa Bay.* www.abcactionnews.com.

Ramsland, Katherine. (2016). *Confession of a serial killer. The untold story of Dennis Rader the BTK killer.* Lebanon, NH. University Press of New England. ForeEdge.

INDEX

OTHER WORKS BY THIS AUTHOR

The Psychopathology of Serial Murder: A Theory of Violence
(1996, Praeger Publishing)

"The Psychopathology of Serial Murder is not a comparison of what is known and it is not to dispel what has been thus far suggested. It is a theory of violence and it is a proficient one, it is believable and comprehendible. I was surprised by this book and believe you will be too. I urge you to get it and place it amongst your most often used resource books—I already have." – serialkillers.net

"Giannangelo makes a good attempt at creating a theory that allows the reader to grasp the data known about serial killers…. Giannangelo skillfully uses this approach to develop the concepts of a serial killer personality, the diagnostic category of 'homicidal pattern disorder,' and a theory of violence." – Journal of the American Academy of Psychiatry and the Law

"I hope you continue contributing to this mystic science. You have one of the clearer voices."
– Jack Olson

Real Life Monsters: A Psychological Examination of the Serial Murderer
(2012, ABC-CLIO)

"I believe that one will leave this book with a better understanding of and increased interest in gaining additional knowledge of the horrific topic of serial murderers—as well as some increased insight into one's own attraction to and repulsion from the frightening phenomenon. The book reads as a lively case discussion with an astute colleague rather than a text or a polemic providing data from an emotional distance." – PsycCRITIQUES

"Giannangelo is among those researchers who accept the complexity of factors involved in the development of these offenders, rather than seeking easy categories or simple answers…. The most riveting part of Real Life Monsters is Giannangelo's interview with an incarcerated serial killer…. It's clear that he sought out someone who was not looking for publicity or selling murderabillia…. This is a serious book."
– Dr. Katherine Ramsland (Shadow Boxing/Psychology Today)

For information about obtaining either book, including a signed copy by the author, please contact me at killerinsights@gmail.com- Stephen J. Giannangelo

www.ingramcontent.com/pod-product-compliance
Lightning Source LLC
Chambersburg PA
CBHW052129270326
41930CB00012B/2820